Copyright © 2017 Karel Murray.

All rights reserved. No portion of this book may be reproduced mechanically, electronically, or by any other means, including photocopying, without written permission of the publisher. It is illegal to copy this book, post it to a website, or distribute it by any other means without permission from the publisher.

Karel Murray
513 SW Station Street
Oak Grove, MO 64075
(816) 400-7120

E-Mail: karel@karel.com
Website: http://www.karel.com

This edition published by

Dog Ear Publishing

4010 W. 86th Street, Ste H

Indianapolis, IN 46268

www.dogearpublishing.net

ISBN: 978-1-4575-5648-7

This book is printed on acid-free paper.

Printed in the United States of America

Limits of Liability and Disclaimer of Warranty

The author and publisher shall not be liable for your misuse of this material. This book is strictly for informational and educational purposes.

Warning—Disclaimer

The purpose of this book is to educate and entertain. The author and/or publisher do not guarantee that anyone following these techniques, suggestions, tips, ideas, or strategies will engender success. The author and/or publisher shall have neither liability nor responsibility to anyone with respect to any loss or damage caused, or alleged to be caused, directly or indirectly by the information contained in this book.

What business professionals say about Karel Murray:

"What stands out about Karel and the presentation – was that it was real. Karel helped the attendees realize and instill a true sense of confidence in themselves and give them courage to battle out whatever challenge they are currently faced with."
Sharon Hoydich, Director of Professional Development, Florida REALTORS®

"Karel Murray's energy and enthusiasm were infectious to the entire audience. Her presentation was very attuned to those in attendance and was humorous, inspirational, and thought provoking."
Jeana Schultz, Urbandale Chamber of Commerce

"Karel Murray is the true master of storytelling and her keynote, The Language of Intent, is a masterpiece. She doesn't just take the audience on her personal journey, but on a meaningful personal journey for each audience member that contains valuable life lessons."
Cindi Ferguson, Professional Development Director, REALTORS® of South Central Kansas

"This woman is absolutely amazing! God has truly blessed her with the ability to reach deep into our emotions and bring sentiment to each situation. Every audience can benefit from Karel's keynote, Language of Intent, because it will have an impact on each attendee in a unique and wonderful way!"
Michelle Ahrens, Director of Education and Dispute Resolutions, REALTOR® Association of the Sioux Empire, Inc.

"Karel is excellent at connecting with her audience and sharing her knowledge in a way that is both very relatable and extremely entertaining. Using her own personal experiences and relevant stories, Karel will help your group gain insight into their own unique situation and provide practical information and strategies to help them be more effective."
Kristen Bechtold, Women in Leadership

From the second I locked eyes with Rick Murray, as he disengaged from a lively conversation with two lovely women, I knew without a doubt I'd just met my life partner, husband, and best friend. In that moment, I understood and embraced without reservation the powerful connections that exist between those we love and others we interact with. This book is dedicated to my husband, who never falters and accepts the world as I see it, without reservations.

Karol Murray

Contents

Introduction		ix
Chapter 1	Language of Science	1
Chapter 2	Language of Self-Created Barriers	3
Chapter 3	Language of Denial	9
Chapter 4	Language of No More	13
Chapter 5	Language of Reality	21
Chapter 6	Language of Belief	27
Chapter 7	Language of Intentional Contentment	37
Chapter 8	Language of Listening and Responding	45
Chapter 9	Language of Action	51
Chapter 10	Language of Leadership	59
Chapter 11	Language of Intent	65
Chapter 12	Observations of Simple Life Rules	73
Unfurl		77
Bonus Pages		79

Introduction

"It's dark down here," I whispered to myself. Swiping a spider web away from my cheek, I pushed myself more closely to the basement stairway wall, huddling as much as I could to ensure my six-year-old body remained out of sight. The pungent meaty smell of the dog food container permeated the air, forcing me to take shallow breaths through my mouth. Having discovered this small space, it became my small haven of security where I could hide from everything but myself.

I learned early what being vulnerable meant, how alone a person can feel, especially when it was self imposed. In the quiet of that childhood basement, I reached for anything that could help me make sense of how the world works as I observed human interaction through television, engaging with spiteful neighborhood children or watching interactions among adults. I huddled in that private place to consider questions way to complex for a six-year old. What causes anger? Is life filled with uncertainty and terror? How can I defend or protect myself from fear? Am I a bad girl and if I am, what made me so? Where does laughter go when the crying starts? Does happiness fade forever or is it possible to bring it back? How can a person love someone deeply but fear them? What am I going to do when I became an adult and will I make a difference?

One day, in the ultimate cocoon of that stairwell, I experienced a comforting sensation that I was not alone. A soft caress of a breeze that shouldn't be there, a feeling of a warm hand on my head urging me to turn my eyes and concentrate on the small patch of light reflecting off the stark white washing machine. A diamond of light that became bleary as my eyes filled with tears.

Comprehension flowed over me. I am not alone.

The knowledge regarding the answers I sought were simple ones. Serenity and resolve grew as I realized I can choose to have control over my reaction to what life hands me – live in the light or surrender to circumstances and dig a hole and bury myself in darkness and depression. The power of intent and self-talk – embodied by a cowed little girl huddling in a corner. Revelation chewed its way through the confusion in my young brain and developed as certainty. I orchestrate the path in my emotional journey.

Understanding, articulating, and vocalizing these lessons have taken me a lifetime. As I look out the window of the home we built for our retirement, I feel compelled to share this sense of continuity, and help others build their foundation of love in the hope that it will not only lessen anxiety but enable others to pass on the legacy of our connection to God.

Ultimately, everything matters. All experiences, interaction, music, art, solitude, life creates the option for us to choose and create our personal manifesto.

The past doesn't matter. The future will unfold regardless of how we may try to control it.

As a teenager, I started envisioning myself as a flexible, unbreakable white wall of resilience. I began accepting what life slams into me, bending to absorb the impact and then snapping back into the shape I choose – not the form others try to mold for me.

I wish that for you.

The Language of Intent is about creating a truthful understanding of the circumstances of our lives and then using everything we can to design the personal reality that brings the best out of us. Our self-talk transforms the outcomes of our lives. It is the greeting of the day that sets actions in motion which ultimately lead to the results we most desire.

To put it simply, don't give in to fate – shape it. The power is within and around you.

Chapter 1: Language of Science
A Layman's Point of View

How on earth do we make sense of the world? Most of us aren't scientists, geologists, historians, environmental engineers, or have advanced degrees in a scientific discipline. Heck, we even have trouble trying to answer the Jeopardy questions Alex Trebek asks on the popular game show! Most of us are trying to earn a living to support ourselves and our families. When we look up into the sky, we see clouds, but may not fully understand the scientific nature of how those clouds came into being. They are simply fluffy and pretty until they turn into a funnel tornado that can threaten our homes and lives. Let the weatherman explain it.

But I realized that defining something doesn't necessarily mean we will understand it. That comes from when the heart and head match the data accumulated, sorting through it to gain clarity and insight. Or we just get another beer and share stories over the fence with the neighbors about the hail that whitened our lawns. It's appropriate to examine some scientific approaches to understanding the fabric of life. Perhaps one will resonate with you.

Quantum theory asserts that a particle is whatever it is measured to be, but that it can't be assumed to have specific properties, or even to exist, until it is measured. Until it is measured, we can't know in what state the object exists. So technically, it exists in all possible states simultaneously, as long as we don't look to check.

The best analogy I came across is rather cruel, but made perfect sense to me. A living cat is placed in a thick airlock box. Suddenly, a person drops in a glass vial of cyanide and slams the lid shut. Until we open the box again, we don't know if the cat is dead because the vial broke open or alive because the vial failed to break. According to quantum law, it is only when we open the box and discover if the cat is dead or alive that we know for sure. For a small space of time, *two* realities exist – one with a live cat, the other with a dead cat.

Many Worlds theory, supported by Stephen Hawking, proposes that parallel universes exit. Each universe has its own reality in which an object can exist. In one world, I could be President of the United States and in another, a homeless person. Mr. Hawking proposes that there is a mechanism for interaction between these universes that somehow permits all states to be accessible in some way and for all possible states to be affected in some manner by our activities in another parallel universe. I loved the novel by Stephen King *11/22/63* which explores this specifically with time travel and impacting (or not) the assassination of John F. Kennedy. Science fiction or reality?

The Secret, a best-selling book written by Rhonda Byrne, explores the concept of the law of attraction. Her focus is emphasizing how positive thinking can create life changing events. The premise is that we have the power to attract wealth, health, or love – that if we visualize what we want and commit our emotions, it happens. Extremely popular, it impacted readers worldwide, which shows me that we, as human beings, want to understand more deeply what is possible. As "The X-Files" Agent Mulder says, "The truth is out there."

We crave something deeper, a profound understanding and meaning to our lives. For some it is through religion, for others volunteerism, in books and movies, or through traveling the globe. And often, no matter how hard we chase it, the "ah ha!" moment escapes us, just when we thought we had it in our grasp. I believe we want the power to shape our lives and control the outcomes from our decisions.

The true problem lies in knowing what that looks like. Without realizing it, we block ourselves with the Language of Self-Created barriers.

Chapter 2: Language of Self-Created Barriers

The genetic code of my birth parents granted me with height and intelligence, and I was born into a family where the Mayor was my father. A nasty combination as a teenager in the 1970s – especially if I wanted to have a boyfriend. Instead, when I stood up, boys had to bend their head back to talk to me. It tended to dampen any romantic endeavors.

I went on my first date in ninth grade. He stood over six feet tall, was a senior, and branded as the school "hood." Glenn wore a letter jacket, had long frizzy hair and rolled Camels in his shirt sleeve – a Brando, one of the wild ones. According to the high school rumor mill, he had a long list of conquests.

I usually intimidated the opposite sex because of my height and my status as the mayor's daughter. I embodied the stereotypical wallflower at teen dances. But then a miracle occurred: Glenn asked me out to the teen dance at the local YMCA. I leapt at the offer. A dance? With a guy taller than me? My loneliness overwhelmed my common sense. The dance awaited my debut.

That Saturday night, I spent hours preparing for the date, choosing a navy dress, short heels borrowed from my mother's closet and nylons – make-up and hair styled to perfection. A winter storm battered the house with ice chips and Arctic air, but I simply glowed with the heat of anticipation. As Glenn pulled up to the house in his jacked-up Camaro, I grabbed the first coat I could from the closet, bypassed boots and raced to the car before he could even shift into park. I didn't ask him in to meet the parents because I knew they would disapprove of him and prevent me from going. Panting, out of breath, I urged him to take off.

As he drove me to the dance, I neared a state of hyperventilation as I pictured myself dancing with him. I thought about all my classmates envying me and how I finally had the chance to show off all those dance moves I had studied for so long.

The Language of Intent

We walked onto the dance floor and the other teens watched us intently. I arrived at a dance with a man, a child no longer. Finally, the ugly duckling became the center of attention and I drank up every envious look. "House of the Rising Sun" by the Animals played over the loudspeakers, Glenn opened his arms and swept me around the floor in practiced moves. Leaning my head into his shoulder, I inhaled his aftershave and gave in to being fully female.

Magic. Simply magic.

While engaged in my incredible first dance, Glenn's friend Allen strolled into the room and pushed his way toward us on the dance floor. He put a restraining hand on Glenn's shoulder and yelled loudly over the music, "Whadyah doin' here with that dog?" Static filled my ears as if a channel on the radio had gone out of tune. Had I heard correctly? Who was he talking about? I thought I looked fierce, elegant, and beautiful. This cruel remark echoed in the air and the other dancers stepped back to take in the show.

Glenn, my perfect first date, scowled, "I know she doesn't look like much, but she's got a nice personality." People started to snicker and whisper behind cupped hands. Allen quickly announced that he thought Glenn had a reputation to protect and should move on. With that statement, my dance partner said, "You're right!" He placed his large hands on my shoulders and shoved. I stumbled backwards and slid to the floor, unable to find anything to halt my fall.

Without a glance back, Glenn retrieved his leather jacket from the folding chair, flung it over his shoulder and joined Allen, heading out the door as all the other teenagers gaped open-mouthed at the drama. He left me there to pick up whatever survived of my pride.

Head hanging, I left the dance floor, trying desperately to ignore the satisfied looks from the other kids. Rather than gain their respect, I somehow earned their derision because of my public rejection. Reaching the front door of the YMCA, I realized I had no money to pay for a taxi and no boots for the 3-mile walk to my home. Too ashamed to call my parents for a ride, I hunched over in the winter wind, while the snow seeped into my shoes. That walk transformed

Chapter 2: Language of Self-Created Barriers

my self-worth from one of budding femininity and love to sheer ugliness. I had been publically rejected by a no-good hood. I might have understood it if he had been a person of quality, but a hood had rejected me. By the time I arrived at my doorstep, I had convinced myself that there really was something wrong with me. My fragile teen self-image had been shattered. From that day forth, nothing I wore looked good enough. I wasn't good enough. For anyone.

A hood had rejected me.

Years later I learned that the scene had been planned. What a fun thing to do: humiliate the mayor's daughter. I think what hurt the most is that not one kid or adult moved to help me or come to my aid. I found it hard to look my peers in the eyes for weeks, feeling the sting of public disdain all around me.

A lot of damage for a first dance.

Beginning in that fragile moment, my flexible white wall (built in that dark basement years before) was transformed into a solid, unmoving brick barrier. I vowed I would trust no one until they earned it over time. I built that wall brick by brick, establishing the barrier that would make sure no person or situation would ever impact me emotionally. Screw everyone and everything. Bitterness settled into a seething disgust, not only for myself, but for the world around me.

The sad part was that it took years for me to realize that my estimation of worth was driven by my own self talk. I did it to myself; I became a self-fulfilling prophecy of negative image.

Desperation for affection and confirmation of self-worth in any form became the strategy of my wounded pride. In a move I'm still surprised at, I entered the first Miss Teenage America Iowa pageant in 1972. I obtained sponsors and donned the white sash and a long ball gown. Pretty elegant for a junior in high school, right? I strutted down the runway, tried to look beautiful, and had an engaging time doing the interviews with the judges. As the winners were announced, they anointed me with the first runner-up position. In an interview I overhead, the judges were asked how they picked between the winner and the first runner-up. The lead judge commented that they felt Karel had a great personality, but the winner had more of an "it" factor.

Huh.

And there it reared its ugly head again – the personality brand. Didn't help that my mother used to tell me, "You won't make it on your looks, so develop an engaging personality. It lasts longer."

Seriously? Who says that? I know she was only trying to toughen me up, to make sure I was prepared emotionally for a grueling life in the business world. But with my already-fragile ego, this did little to boost my confidence.

Did Glenn and Allen do me a favor years before in confirming my mother's words? I realized that maybe all I had was personality, so I would just roll with it. Our greatest fear is centered around the mortification of having others witness our rejection, regardless of the form it takes. We pray it doesn't occur in front of others. Unfortunately, rejection has a way of finding a public arena in which to present itself. The idea that our actions or decisions are being discussed by others over coffee or on the phone hovers over our mental well-being. Ultimately, this feeling of inadequacy and embarrassment invades our everyday lives. Thus, we create barriers to ensure rejection doesn't happen.

Play it safe.

The type of emotional upheaval I experienced at the dance can drive people to run home, crawl into bed, and throw the covers over their heads.

Those who love us have a way of short-circuiting our dreams with their constant reminders that we aren't going to get what we strive for. We may never see a glimpse of that parallel world of "what if." Why do we allow others to determine our self-esteem? Shame on us. The Language of Self-Created Barriers puts others in a position of power to harm us.

Look within yourself to see where your negative self-talk began to seep into your thoughts and perception of your ability or achievements. Identify who the vipers are in your life and evaluate the amount of control you have allowed them over your choices and attitude. One of the wisest people I know, my sister Kendall, told me years ago that no one has the power to make us unhappy unless we permit it. We all have human frailties, and we will take rejection personally, but I encourage you to try and step back and analyze the situation objectively. Look for ways to make rejection work to your advantage. For example, some of the world's great comedians use their own pain and embarrassment to make us laugh; we recognize and release the pain of our own rejection experiences as we listen to their stories.

Understand the "animal" you are interacting with. Do your research. Determine what the logic is behind the other person's motivation. Build a level of tolerance for change. If you understand emotionally and intellectually the other person's perspective, you can work with it more effectively. The goal is to minimize blindsided reactions.

Picture this: you come upon a rattlesnake (or co-worker) ready to strike. You think you're a goner. But let's back up. You have entered their territory and it's your responsibility to pay attention to the landscape and recognize warning signs of a potential strike: intimidating questions, impatience, aggressive eye contact, curtness, or body language that places you on the defensive. Are the wagons circled and are you on the outside? Be ready to protect yourself and then utilize the right self-talk to change the outcome of the interaction to either deflect or neutralize the threat or at least minimize the impact of the attack.

Work aggressively to have integrity in your own self-management.

Don't feed drama. It only strengthens your personal barriers, possibly to the point where you are once again in that dark basement, wondering why you are there in the first place. You and you alone make the decision to run back to that dark corner.

It takes time for us to figure out that cause and effect is built over years of repeated behaviors. By creating options and applying the right emotional energy to accomplish something positive we regain our equilibrium. Look around you. Life bubbles over – it is vast and filled with so many levels of joy, diversity, anger, and confusion.

How complex do you want to make your life? You can choose. You control more than you can possibly know. But this is all worthless unless we get past the Language of Denial.

Chapter 3: Language of Denial

Children have an incredible ability to look at life without filters. What they see and hear is real. No second guessing about hidden meanings or spending time in long evaluations regarding the whys relating to the situation. I knew my mother was furious when she discovered I had plucked the ivory keys off the baby grand piano and used permanent colored markers to make an ivory deck of cards out of the piano keys. At age five, I thought it a creative use of my unsupervised time and believed I had made the piano look exceptionally cool. Little did I realize I had vandalized a family treasure. Cause and effect became very clear very quickly.

As we grow up, the use of denial and applying filters on our behavior intensifies. We often do everything in our power to rationalize the what, where, when, and how of life as it unfolds. Limiting our willingness to look deeply at something creates our personal Language of Denial. If we don't see it, it isn't real. If we can't imagine what might be possible, it will never happen. Thus, we act out situations in our lives repeatedly, in the same way with the same results.

A sobering thought – especially when we know we are in a dark place and desperate to get out.

At an early age, I learned I have an ear for music. When I was four, my parents woke up early one morning thinking the radio was playing the theme song of the movie, "The Longest Day." When they stumbled out into the living room, they witnessed me playing the song on the piano. Perched against the chair, one foot on a pedal, my fingers flew over the keys in perfect rhythm. My mother, who loved to sing, thought I could live her interrupted dream of a music career. My sister, Kendall, encouraged me to listen to the music of the sixties, which had such diversity in melodies and lyrics. My young heart swelled at the thought of such beauty in the world.

I love music and understand it at a subatomic level. It resides in my DNA.

When I was around seven, my mother sent me to a local piano teacher for lessons. Instructed to nurture my perceived raw ability into a structured talent, she began the aggressive lessons. We started with learning to read sheet music, what the notes meant, how they looked and how they were to be played. The teacher would demonstrate on the piano each bar of written music and then have me repeat what she did. She never figured out that I was ignoring the sheet music. I simply listened and watched what she did when she played and then repeated it. I believed I already knew how to play and thus denied myself the ability of taking my talent to the next level.

If I missed a key, her sharp retort made me cringe. Playing music became a chore, something to dread. My original joy in creating music turned into anxiety. After four years of lessons, a piano recital was held for parents. When I took my seat on the stool, my heart surged against my chest and I found it hard to keep my fingers from trembling. The first chord launched one of the most disastrous events of my life. The look of anger on the teacher's face and confusion on my parents' faces made the completion of the song impossible. I pushed away from the piano and ran.

This embarrassing event blossomed into a toxic cloud of self-doubt. One messed up recital and I effectively self-talked myself into believing I couldn't play in front of people. My stage fright playing a musical instrument became an established fact of my life.

Purchasing a steel string guitar, I used this wonderful instrument to accompany me when I sang at weddings. The only caveat – I had to sing from the balcony where people couldn't see me and I needed the words in front of me. Shortly after I was married, a friend asked me to sing at her wedding. Stationed in the balcony, I was to begin the song after the church bells rang 12 times. On the 12th ring, my friend and her father would begin their processional accompanied by my song.

Chapter 3: Language of Denial

Wearing a flowing medieval frock, guitar slung over my shoulder, I made myself ready. Guitar – check. Husband behind me – check. Words to the song – missing. A complete disaster in the making.

I frantically clawed through my purse; no sheet of paper with the words. I grabbed my husband and searched his pockets; no words to the song. The church bell started to peal.

On the 3rd ring, I shoved my husband to the stairway and hissed at him to stop the wedding! Stop the bells! I couldn't sing without the words! 9th ring, hands sweating, I clutched the fret of the guitar, fingers on the strings, praying the words would come to me.

12th ring of the bells, no husband, no words and silence prevailed over the hushed congregation as everyone waited for me to begin.

I struck the first chord – a wrong key.

I attempted the note again – wrong chord. Dear God, how was this possible? Panic locked my vocal chords.

I leaned over the balcony, cringing and croaked, "Sorry! I'll begin again." Gulping, shaking, I breathed deeply, found the right chord and played gently. Once the first line of the song filled the church, I calmed down and sang without further incident.

Afterwards, my gracious friend came up to hug me. She whispered in my ear that at least her wedding would be memorable! Flushed and embarrassed, I couldn't believe how she could make light of something so disastrous.

It floored me. That's when I realized that the earth, moon, and stars didn't revolve around whether I did a song well or not. It simply isn't a life altering event.

That event began my journey of understanding the language of denial and how it can halt a beautiful possibility before it even begins.

After 10 years of marriage, I finally bought a full-sized electronic keyboard and began to write the music that had been simmering in my head over the years. Obviously, I couldn't *write* music since I had no idea how to *read* music. I created a shorthand that only I could read. Stress grew as I realized that the piano played only one dimension of what I heard in my head and soul. I couldn't introduce the French horns, drums, strings into the melody. When I played my music, listeners heard only the piano and not the richness of the orchestral harmony intertwined with the melody.

I informed Rick that I needed a sequencer (equipment that will play other instruments and embed the sound within the track of music I created) and computer software that writes the sheet music as I play it. Softly he asked, "This is very expensive. Do you plan on making a living at music to warrant the purchase?"

Defeated, I sighed, "No."

Three weeks later I sold the keyboard. If I couldn't write what I heard in my head, I didn't want to proceed. My Language of Denial was so strong that it convinced me that 75% of something wasn't good enough. If I couldn't be the best or do my best, I won't do it at all.

I denied myself growth and personal challenge. I did that. No one else.

I became a master of keeping my head down, working hard to pass unnoticed unless I wanted to be seen. I easily wrapped the cloak of isolation around me. Little did I know that this self-imposed garment gained weight, stifling me at every swing of the hem. I essentially denied myself curiosity regarding other people and opportunities, choosing instead to play it safe and focus on my internal development.

Thank God, life has a way of waking us up. Enter the Language of No More…

Chapter 4: Language of No More

Rage against the storm. You know the image – a sailor floundering at sea, boat hull shuddering from the impact of thunderous waves and the howl of a wind so fierce it resembles the scream of a murderous animal. He clings to the mast, face upturned, jaw locked in a rictus of defiance, shrieking, "YOU WILL NOT WIN!" The surge of the storm clashes with the will of the small, inconsequential being and we hold our breath. Who will prevail?

What must happen before we wake up?

What do we need to lose, break, find, experience, or kill before we regain control over our own existence? I remember the Star Wars movies and the Jedi Masters. The battle to gain "the Force" was a battle from within – a battle of conquering the demons we hold and nurture inside.

Using images from a powerful film might help you understand where I am trying to lead you. The movie "The Elephant Man" changed my perspective completely. It told the true story of Joseph Carey Merrick, deformed by hideous tumors on his face and body, found at a freak show by a medical doctor. The scene that still brings tears to my eyes shows John Merrick lurching through a train station, shrouded in a dark cloak and a hood shielding his eyes. People at the station stare and him then proceed to follow him, chasing him through the station and causing his hood to fall back and reveal his frightening face. He is cornered at a gate that blocks an exit. The crowd shoves him, screams at him, and John finally howls, "I am not an animal! I am not an animal!"

At what point do we scream, "No More"?

What type of experience does it take to transform our thinking and determination? At what point do we look to *what is possible* rather than accept *what is* our fate or probable path to self-destruction?

The Language of Intent

Everyone has their breaking point and that isn't necessarily a bad thing. I believe that a breaking point is when we finally wake up and take a stand. We choose: the easy way or the hard way. We give in to circumstances we can't control and begin laying plans for what lies next. Our decisions help us maintain the resiliency of a tide: a powerful repetitive action that ultimately brings calm internally as we watch the surf break, knowing another wave will soon follow. Nature's persistence is a lesson we can all learn.

However, our world view can change without warning. An event or experience forces us to look inside and find our strength. Let me share two examples.

My husband, Rick, is a red-haired Scotsman. Tall, chiseled Gaelic features and trimmed beard complement his gentle, caretaking personality. Working in Missouri as an agricultural chemical representative for a large national firm, Rick provided competent, exceptional service appreciated by his customers. Without warning, we learned he had skin cancer, which appeared as a large growth over his right ear, under his short red hair. A section the size of a tennis ball had to be excised from the area and a skin graft from his thigh completed the operation. The resulting scar will never grow hair.

Rick dealt with this calmly, understanding it as a fact of life we can't do anything about. But, the scar, so prominent, needed to be addressed. The only alternative: grow his hair long into a ponytail. It transformed the way he looked but his personality and drive remained the same.

We moved to a farming community in Iowa because of a company transfer. Rick went to work meeting with farmers and coops, one-on-one and in groups. To Rick, it was the normal course of business. He noticed the looks from conservative farmers as they glanced at his pony tail, but thought nothing of it. At least, not until "the meeting."

In a gathering of 20+ company managers and peers, Rick was to make a formal presentation regarding the chemical offerings that would work for their next year's crops. Prior to and during his presentation, murmuring went through the crowd, sniggers, and

Chapter 4: Language of No More

pointed fingers. Whispered comments about his beard and pony tail assaulted him throughout the day. Finally, Rick was informed that he needed to re-evaluate his appearance to conform to the company norm. If he didn't understand that, he was obviously in the wrong place.

As Rick tells the story, every possible emotion, from being stunned, to ashamed, to angered surged through him. Why would these people be acting like this? He was the same man he was in Missouri – professional, competent, and kind. What did he do to deserve this?

With heavy silence and disappointment, Rick met privately with several key players in his company. With each individual, he reached up, pulled out the elastic band from his hair and let his long auburn hair fall about his face. It parted to show the glaringly white scar over his right ear. He pointed at the scar and quietly asked, "Tell me, how would you cover up this scar I got because of skin cancer?"

Shamed, the men looked down at their laps. Rick tied his hair back up into the pony tail and murmured to himself, "I thought so."

When he returned home, he sat at the table with such a defeated, angry, confused look on his face that it broke my heart. At that moment, I saw such a resolution in his eyes. He would not be a victim anymore for anyone. In the next 18 months, he made one of the worst territories in the country into number one in the world and was awarded an international award as top salesperson for his efforts.

Nothing would stop him – cancer, people, or circumstance. He will fight until he can't.

It is my honor to learn from him every day. He has made me a better person by example. But watching and realizing what you are made of is different for each of us.

As I withdrew into my own world as a form of self-protection, I didn't get involved in other people's issues. I did my work and

15

went home. Safe and sound from life's drama. All that changed on a crystalline winter day: January 22, 1988.

I started a new career in Pittsburgh, Pennsylvania. It was an exciting time and a wonderful opportunity for me as I assumed the role of a regional administrative manager in an insurance company located in downtown Pittsburgh. Every day, I had to ride the commuter train, disembark, and walk six blocks to my office.

To keep me warm during these walks, my husband purchased a full-length beaver coat as a Christmas present. I didn't look out of place, as many other career women taking the same stroll each winter day wore the same thing. Just another busy, warm person striding on her way to work. I fell in love with Pittsburgh and all it had to offer.

On Friday, January 22, 1988, at 7:00 AM, I wound my way through the busy foot traffic, hustling to my office. The gusting winds blew sharp needles of ice against my face and snow impeded my distance vision. Any slush on the ground quickly froze – a treacherous morning. Standing at a stop light of a four-lane street, I glanced across at the group waiting to cross over to the other side. Among the sharply dressed women, my eyes settled on an elderly gentleman, filthy dirty, unshaven, torn clothing, weaving on his feet. He leaned against the light pole, sighing.

Dismay filled me as I realized I was probably looking at an inebriated street person. It's so early in the morning! I decided I wouldn't look at this person… just ignore him and continue my way. The light changed and I began my crossing with a score of other individuals. Moving forward on the slippery ice, jostled by someone from behind, I turned my head and stared directly into the eyes of the homeless man.

We locked gazes – riveted in time.

The clarity and intense blue of his irises as well as the soulful calm and forgiveness in his eyes blessed me. I almost stumbled in surprise. I truly believed I had gazed into the eyes of an angel. So compelling was his look, that when I reached the other side, I turned around to look once again to confirm what I had witnessed.

Chapter 4: Language of No More

I froze in shock.

Across the busy four lane street, I saw a crumpled form on the pavement, about 10 feet from the curb. Blood was running from his mouth and beginning to freeze to the pavement. An arm turned at an impossible angle and snow already beginning to create a light dusting of white over the still form.

But it wasn't this image that made me start shouting and pointing. A sea of people had parted around the man, and no one stopped. A sidelong glance was the most attention he received.

Rationally, I could understand their total lack of involvement because of the AIDS scare. In 1988, we were just beginning to learn about the issues related to the transmission of the disease and touching tainted blood might put a person at risk. However, emotionally, I saw this man, in pain and obvious jeopardy, being ignored like road kill.

Shrieking, I ran back across the four lanes of traffic once the light changed and slid to my knees beside the still form. Those eyes… He looked at me in complete peace and kindness as if to say, "Ah…. there you are." My heart clenched and my anger at the crowd faded. I gently asked him if he could move his neck because I had to put my coat under his head to prevent his skin from freezing to the sidewalk. He carefully nodded. I stripped off my new fur coat and gently placed it under his head.

Assessing the glaze of sweat on his face, I realized shock could set in. His face, extremely pale and his erratic breathing became a great concern. I clutched at a passing commuter and asked him for his coat to drape over the man. He stopped immediately and handed me his wool duster. Another man offered his jacket which I gladly accepted. Next I shouted to a woman to call 911. She raced away into the nearest commercial building for a telephone. By this time, there were nearly two dozen people gathered around me and the injured man. (I later learned there were exactly 22 people in that group.)

17

As I shivered over the man, a dark-haired woman called out to the others and suggested that they create a tight circle, shoulder to shoulder, hip to hip, and surround the two of us so that the wind could be blocked effectively.

They did this without hesitation. Their generous spirit became a testament to our human capacity to help our own.

The paramedics arrived about 10 minutes later. They quickly and efficiently lifted the man onto a gurney and placed him inside the ambulance. Catching the attention of a young medic, I gave my card to him and requested an update on the man's condition later in the day. The entire time, the angel's eyes never left my face and his expression of peace and forgiveness touched me to my very core.

One by one, the people in our protective circle came up and handed me their business cards, all asking for an update on the man's condition, which I was happy to do. My new coat, spattered with blood, created quite a stir when I showed up at the office.

Later that day, the medic called. He reported that this man worked in the steel mills at night. During that time in Pittsburgh, steel operations were shutting down and this was the only work he could find. The man, 68 years old, unable to survive on his Social Security, worked on a cleaning crew. That day, on his way home, he felt usually tired. He had taken a cold tablet and it hit him a bit hard – enough to make him dizzy. Thus, leaning on the traffic light gave him the much-needed support. The medic informed me that the man had fractured his jaw, but his arm had no breaks; it was just severely twisted. The man's biggest concern centered on his ability to pay his bills as he healed over the next few months.

After the call, I phoned everyone who had helped that morning. By 10:00 AM the next day, these people had donated enough money to take care of any bills not covered by Medicare as well as to help him live for months – covering rent and utilities. We worked through the medic to make sure the injured man received the fund. The medic wanted to share the story with the local newspapers, but we had all agreed that we were to remain anonymous.

Chapter 4: Language of No More

I have thought often about that day, knowing that somehow this incident liberated me. We all have those times in our lives – experiences that mean we can't turn back. We are left with a sense of new understanding and permission to act differently.

Be different without regret or recrimination.

That day, the man's situation tested me and I had passed my own personal trial. In a moment of pure instinct, I burst through my barriers of denial and self-doubt by simply acting. No second guessing about what others might think of me.

What experiences have finally pushed you to the edge where you decided to act or flee? How have others reached out to you in your time of need? When did you decide you were ready to be of service – determined to reject your need for isolation and make it your mission to act when action is called for regardless of personal stress that might come to you?

In that moment with the fallen angel, I became receptive to the Language of No More and how to live in the spaces between universes. What is reality other than what we perceive it to be? Can coincidences be rewritten as fate? The truth of our connections to each other continue to astound me.

Twenty years later, during an ethics class in Des Moines, Iowa, I began telling the story about the man who fell in Pittsburgh, tying it into a concept we were discussing. At the end of the story, a student requested loudly that I allow a break. Thinking that this had emotionally impacted her, I dismissed the students for ten minutes.

The first words out of the student's mouth was "Did this happen on January 22, 1988?"

I said, "Yes."

She then identified the Pittsburgh cross streets where the incident occurred. How on earth could she know this? Is she psychic since I hadn't mentioned either the exact date or the streets in my storytelling session? Her eyes teared up and she hugged me.

19

With her mouth muffled in my shoulder, she said, "I moved here from Pittsburgh. I've always wanted to meet you! My cousin was the paramedic called to the scene. He had never seen anything like this ring of people surrounding a coatless woman and an old man, sheltering them from the wind and snow. The level of cooperation from the bystanders – incredible! He also said that you and the others refused to allow him to tell the media. My cousin says they had put up a "salute" in the precinct to "The 22," as you and the others are considered the angels of that corner by the paramedic group!"

My breath catches every time I think of her; because of our very human, unplanned but caring response, 22 people had risen to "angel" status. By helping someone we thought was a wounded angel, we became angels ourselves.

Think about your perception of the world around you. What will it take to open your eyes and understand what has been in front of you all your life?

There is power in clarity and a personal understanding of the whys in your life when you embrace the Language of Reality.

Chapter 5: Language of Reality

It is the weirdest feeling in the world... the lack of control. I've experienced it before when my son, Ben, was 2 years old and launched a screaming tantrum in the toy department. He commanded attention from every passing mother, pleading his case for a new toy. His small grasping hands reaching out pitifully, his clenched eyes, his wide open mouth howling his dismay was almost enough to do me in. What kind of a mother would deny her beautiful baby what his heart desires?

Obviously...me.

Of course, I had options. I could have gathered him up, tucked him under my arm, kicking and screaming, and marched out of the store. But, doing that would have denied me the pleasure of finishing a much-needed shopping spree. So, I sat on the floor, placing myself at his eye level, and quietly waited for him to finish. He was a determined little bugger. For almost seven minutes, he screeched his indignation, red faced, tears streaking down his innocent cheeks. Other parents looked at me quickly, shared a brief smile of support, and moved to another isle, hustling their children before them, hoping they wouldn't get any ideas from Ben's rebellion.

Do you have any idea how long seven minutes is with a shrieking child?

A lifetime.

I sat resolutely, with a calm, patient look on my face, personally praying for earplugs. Putting my fingers in my ears didn't seem like the adult thing to do. Finally, the tantrum dried up. He stuck his fingers in his mouth, sniffled, and came over to sit on my crossed legs. A heavy sigh leaked from his tired throat and he nestled into the crook of my arm. A gentle hug told him all was forgiven, but reinforced that Momma had control.

That was in the 1980's. In today's world, I probably would have been ushered out of the store by management, chastened by other parents for child abuse, or been forced to explain myself to the authorities for the noise pollution.

As we age, when someone challenges us, we realize that we can only respond with a shrug.

I don't know about you, but I can only see the world through my experiences, my perspective shaped by circumstances unique to me. When I'm startled, I jump. This usually scares the daylights out of people who sit with me in a movie theater. When I watch soldiers moving down the jet way from a plane and surging into the arms of their families, I cry.

Personally, I think the world is almost too real, as we are accosted by local, national, and world news on a 24-hour basis anywhere we might be. We can try to shut out the noise, but in our minds that nasty voice whispers, "What if you miss something important?" This continual state of being "plugged in" creates awareness of issues others are facing and raises commiserating stress in equal measure. With so much vicarious involvement with others' lives, we need to allow ourselves a chance to laugh at fate, or at least at adversity, so that we can regain our footing.

I have learned that the best humor moments are when I get real – speaking the truth that everyone is thinking. For the last 15 years, I've been a large woman, gaining weight and moving up the dress size chart, making excuses for the bodily changes every way I could. Scheduled to present a motivational keynote at a national convention, I wore a flowing outfit that unfortunately emphasized my size.

I stood at the back of the auditorium as directed by the meeting planner. Suddenly, down the center aisle, six beautiful, slim young girls wearing skimpy cheerleading outfits danced and skipped up to the stage. These lovelies waved their pom poms, jumped in the air, and generally shook every beautiful part of their bodies. Mortified, I realized that this production was the meeting planner's way of presenting me to the 500 audience members.

Chapter 5: Language of Reality

My introduction boomed throughout the room, and I warily walk up on stage. I thanked the executive and turned to look at the cheerleaders on the stage. I didn't speak for a minute – just stared mutely at them, then the audience.

I walked over to each cheerleader and lined them up on the stage so that one girl stood at the front and the others lined up behind her. I then walked to the front of the line and asked the audience "Are they gone? Can you see them anymore?" Which, of course, they couldn't. The howl of laughter that erupted from the attendees still makes me smile today.

Or what about following a speaker who leaps up on the stage like a gazelle, doing flips, and delivering a motivational talk at the same time? How do I follow that? Simple – I walked out on the platform, laid down on the floor, crossed my arms and rolled. The startled response from the audience at this silly act brought the house down - memories of being a kid rolling down a neighborhood hill used effectively as a mechanism for humor. That day, I got real. I'm an older woman, overweight, and there is no way I can compete on an uneven playing field with a physically endowed athlete.

I use the moment of reality and play with it. I don't try to overcome something I can't change. I reformat the conversation.

Reality has a way of hitting us right in the face when we least expect it. I moved through my life believing that I had unlimited time to do everything I dreamed up. Then, I learn my twin brother, Kevin, is stricken with ALS. This horrifying disease dismantled his physical control, one system at a time, until his death at age 61 on March 22, 2016.

We grieved his passing, but I wasn't prepared for the other emotions sneaking in: I started to become focused on my own mortality. My twin had died. And I am still here. An irrational fear morphed into a realization that I had not taken care of my body. I pushed past the excuses that had supported a hefty weight gain and looked coldly into the mirror at my naked form.

The Language of Reality in full unflinching view. If I couldn't/wouldn't love my body, why should expect to have a pain-free retirement?

Pushing aside negative, indoctrinated self-talk, I crushed the excuses and grabbed onto the belief that my health is within my control. I ignored all my past failures to exercise, control my diet, and increase daily activity. I shook off the expectation that just because I am in my sixties, I had to accept the life of a woman in decline.

I decided that there was no reason *not* to take control.

The Language of Reality is vital. It keeps us in the frame of an accurate picture: what we are doing, where we are going, and how the achievement of our goals is shaping up. Otherwise, we could be making plans for our life based upon wrong data.

I had to get accurate information. The journey had to begin with a personal, self-directed inventory of my medical status.

In November 2016, I had the following exams/tests/procedures:

- Bloodwork to benchmark status for cholesterol, sugars, etc.
- MRI of the lower spine

    Degeneration of lower back – inoperable.

    Steroid injections to the lower back to reduce the swelling around the discs.

    Met with a sports medicine specialist who set up physical therapy and established an exercise regime to strengthen my core.
- Underwent auditory tests to measure hearing deterioration
- Eyes examined
- Allergy testing for environmental and food allergies

Discovered my body is inflamed due to allergies related to almost everything – environmental and food related.

Routine visits with a nutritionist with menu that eliminates the severest allergy impacted foods, which included: eggs, wheat, milk, sugars, all carbs.

- Calcium screening of the heart

December 1, 2016 – I examined all the results objectively, under a harsh light, and activated a yearlong health program.

May 2017 – I have lost 35 pounds (of my 70-pound goal); my cholesterol and sugar levels dropped by 75%; I dropped four clothing sizes, my back doesn't hurt; and as I walk on the tread mill for 30 minutes I am grinning like an idiot. I visualize my healthiest self and what that looks like. I laughed out loud when a friend of mine suggested that I don't lose too much weight and start to look old.

What is our aging reality? As we enter the retirement phase of our lives we must get emotionally prepared for it. Our attitude and approach to aging can be transformed into curiosity and growth. Sure, body parts are drifting south, a strand of gray hair appears, and eyesight isn't anything to brag about… But we are entering a world of possibilities where reality happens and all we can do is hang on for the ride!

It's our self-talk that sets the stage for the quality of our daily existence. Listen to what you are saying to yourself and evaluate it closely. Are you driven to lamenting all that you have lost or have you redirected your self-talk into the arena of understanding the cycle of life?

The Language of Reality is just pure fact – nothing covers up the flaws. How we deal with information is what separates us into those who find contentment and those who rage against whatever can't be controlled.

The Language of Intent

Scars of our past are visible and ready for examination. Explore your nature and own it.

Once you have the fortitude to own what is real in your life, you open the door to the Language of Belief and begin making your intentions take form and purpose.

Chapter 6: Language of Belief
A Leap of Faith

An argument can be made that we can't get something just by believing it is possible. For example, I can't become a millionaire just by believing the next lottery ticket will be "the one."

But my husband knows that *someone* must win, so why not him? Now that is the Language of Belief in full force.

> **There comes a point in our lives where instinct, information and belief collide. It is called a leap of faith.**

Belief takes so many forms – mental, physical, and spiritual. Much of the world's population is aligned with a specific religion, with rituals and actions embracing fundamental truths that describe what lies beyond. For most of my adult life, I couldn't understand why religion existed – the premise of God and enlightenment, that someone exists in the great beyond that we reach to attain through the actions of our lives on earth. I simply couldn't understand why there were so many ways to express that belief until a friend of mine shared what her Buddhist grandmother explained to her.

Envision a mountain leveled off at the top. At the plateau, all understanding, love, joy, and peace reside alongside God. A place of communion, contentment, and worth. Each religion has chosen a side of the mountain on which they climb to reach the top. Each face and overcome the hurdles of the terrain they encounter. All religions want to achieve the plateau; they strive for the same outcome. They simply take different paths to that enlightenment.

In my many late-night talks with my mother, I learned that she believed in connections between life and death. I came to believe that love transcends all barriers. No science to it, just an inner foundation of strength in making decisions based upon instinct that is ignited by our angels or God.

I continued my "education" working as a hospice volunteer where I engaged in many spiritual conversations with those who were on their last journey. We discussed things like:

- What if God is every person?

- What if we truly opened ourselves to what is possible in order to feel that energy when we interact or touch?

- What if we withhold judgement and reservation and accept what we feel at a visceral level?

- Is everything in life relative to the experiences and actions you take?

- What is the spark that leads to intuition?

Think back to those times where you knew someone meant you harm (emotionally or physically), but you chose to override that feeling and then were hurt as a direct result. Have you met someone for the first time and felt that you have known them forever? Had an uncanny certainty that directs the decisions you make?

Everything we are, how we express ourselves, and the decisions we make may be assisted by the energy of those who are foundational in our lives, living and dead. How often have you prayed for guidance and support from a parent who has passed away and felt a wave of comfort like the warm embrace you used to share?

Let me walk you through the series of events which led to my absolute belief in the space between life and death: a highly personal and private pact made with my dying father. The dimension of that connection transcends my understanding and to this day demands the suspension of denial.

My father passed away in 1988. Two weeks before he died, I stayed with him at the hospital, sleeping on a cot at the side of his hospital bed. My mother collapsed at home, exhausted from the vigil, regaining the strength she would need once Dad was released from life.

Chapter 6: Language of Belief

I knew my father as a consummate professional, even within the confines of our relationship. He embodied a person I could trust, but I didn't have the ability to break past his barriers and learn about the "personal" side of my father. He was Dad and that was enough.

Lucid to the end, my father kept family and friends at a distance, even though he was facing the biggest event of his life. On my last afternoon visit with him, my husband and young son sat off to the side and allowed me a private moment to say goodbye.

Unexpectedly, Dad whispered softly, "I'm afraid, Karel. I have no idea what to expect."

I cradled his hand in mine and bent over to speak to him. His eyes locked onto a corner of the room while a gentle smile played over his emaciated face. He raised his other hand and waved it in the air saying, "Not now, Mom, I need to talk to her."

I held my breath. He was seeing and speaking to his mother, who had died many years before.

Dad returned his eyes to me and said, "I wasn't a good father to you and for that I'm sorry. I promise that I'll be a much better father after I die than when I was alive. I'll watch over you, always." Under that resolute gaze, I believed him and accepted the gift he offered. Smiling broadly, I replied with the utmost seriousness, "Dad, I know you will. But first I have some rules for you to follow. Is that okay?"

He nodded and I continued, "First – you are never allowed to visit me in the master bedroom – that is private." He gave me a look of amusement and promised. "Second – you are not allowed to hang out in the bathroom when I am using it – that is private." Dad's smile broadened. "Finally, Dad, you are not allowed to jump out of a closet and scare the crap out of me!" At that he laughed out loud. We shook on the promise.

If you haven't guessed by now, humor is the way I deal with high stress situations. My father understood and graced our last moments together with laughter.

I was back at home in Pittsburgh two weeks later when my husband left for a business trip. Before dawn on the day of my father's passing, I woke up to the urging of my Dad.

A powerful dream? How did he get in the room?

As I sat up on the side of the bed, I smelled cherry tobacco smoke, which was the kind of pipe tobacco Dad smoked all his life. I waited, then slowly let out my breath. I hadn't realized I had been holding it.

He was gone. Five minutes later, a family member called me to let me know he had just died. A contact beyond comprehension or possibility? Or is the spark of God so strong it seeps through any barrier with a strong enough will?

For years, I kept this experience between my husband and myself along with the hospital conversation and his caress at his death. It brought me comfort beyond what one would consider rational. It simply existed as a pact that would be honored.

Move forward 15 years.

The year – 2003. It was a morning like all others. The sun shone brightly as I cruised in the far-left lane of six-lane Highway 70 on my way to Kansas City from Blue Springs, Missouri. I glanced in the rear-view mirror and noticed a huge semi-tractor trailer traveling at top speed in my lane. Suddenly, without warning, I heard in my head my Dad screaming "Pull over to the right side and stop NOW!"

I acted immediately, with absolutely no thought of why I was doing this strange thing. I pulled over quickly, slammed on the brakes and came to a completely stop. The semi blew past me, still in the left lane and rear ended a red SUV. Then all hell broke loose, cars tumbling, swerving, crumbling from impacts because of 30+ cars being out of control during rush hour. The semi buckled as it crashed into the other vehicles.

I watched in horror as cars spun around me. But not one hit me as I idled on the side of the road in the only "clear" spot on the highway, one vehicle slammed to a stop two feet behind me and another three yards in front. Grabbing my cell phone, I dialed 911, reported the multi-car accident and gave my statement. They told me to leave the scene and emergency vehicles were on their way and would be there in minutes. Shaken, I took the exit and drove to my appointment.

My father saved my life. I don't know how, but I believe.

Years later, after sharing this story, I met a young woman who informed me that the semi driver was her father. He had left home that morning intending to kill as many people as he could. Her father is currently serving his sentence in prison for his actions.

How is it possible that the first day I reveal this secret I've held for years is told at a time when another person is in the room who was also personally impacted by the event? Is it coincidence or fate? Were we meant to meet that day and help each other find meaning and redemption?

The more we look outside ourselves, the easier it is to recognize those moments of clarity and connection. Our self-talk and belief in what is possible provides us a platform for incredible possibilities and opportunity.

How is it possible that we can be given the gift of time?

While I was making a presentation in Philadelphia, my sister called and told me my mother was being transferred to Hospice and was not expected to live much longer. I desperately needed a month to be with her, before and after her death. Within 48 hours, my next four speaking engagements were rescheduled, not by me, but at the initiation of my clients.

The Language of Intent

In my dismay, I thought only "How on earth do I fix this?" Somehow, I reached out to the universe and sent my "intent," calling upon whoever was listening for help.

The universe responded. And I believed.

For me, it took years of weaving one incident into another that crystalized my understanding of our connection to God and to others.

Consider how you have created your belief system. What must be in place before you finally look up and say, "I'm ready to commit fully and completely. That personal act of laying all your cards on the table and declaring I'm all in!" Those moments come at the strangest times. For me they came at a time when my need to share what I know was becoming more urgent.

It came in the form of an unexpected appointment with a medium scheduled by my best friend without my knowledge.

The blue wood door opened to reveal a brown-haired woman of about my age. Wearing jeans and flowing white shirt, she oozed confidence. She graciously accepted that I was to be her client instead of my friend and led me up the stairs to her salon. After she had settled in her chair, she advised me that she would be meditating and reaching out to those who wanted to "talk" to me.

Okay then.

Sensing how easily barriers can be crossed, it still caused me some anxiety to be in the presence of someone who talks to the dead. I'd seen way too many movies.

After a few moments of heavy silence, she gave a knowing nod of head and opened her eyes, looking deeply into mine. "Your father is here. His name is Ken and he died in 1988."

What? How on earth can this woman know this? She didn't even know I was coming that day! My father's name was Ken and she had the year of his death correct. I requested validation that she was truly talking to my dad, so I asked, "What was the promise he made to me?"

The medium lowered her head, nodded again and said without looking up, "He promised to be a better father to you after his death than when he was alive. He wants to know if you have felt his presence."

I told her that I had always known he was with me, but asked her to have him tell me how he has reached out. She paused, concentrated, then replied, "He yelled at you to get off the road because the semi was going to rear-end you."

My throat closed with emotion, almost panic. How this was possible? Finally, asking for the ultimate confirmation of her ability, I requested that she tell me what "The Rules" were.

Once again, her head drifted towards her chest. Then a brilliant smile broke through her solemn demeanor and she laughed out, "You are kidding me! Karel, your Dad says he isn't to be in your bedroom or bathroom because they are private places and not to jump out of a closet and scare the daylights out of you! He has never broken those promises."

At that moment, I became a solid believer in the God Connection.

The medium then declared that the space around me was crowded with angels, urging me to speak truth, share the message that needed to be told. My angels, according to the medium, insisted I had to make the decision to write my truth and trust that thousands will hear it and find peace and hope.

This meeting, unexpected and unplanned, began the path for The Language of Intent. But a piece of me still suspended going "all in" on belief. I kept the door shut and played it safe.

Until the summer of 2016.

You know those types of days that are so hot the car windows steam over when the air conditioning is turned on? Where exposed door handles sear the fingerprints off the tips of each digit, so a quick clutching maneuver must be used as a preventive measure against a burn?

That day, I truly dreaded getting into the vehicle, knowing that the interior would feel like a vacuum, sucking the life energy out of every pore of my body. The shriek that followed when my thighs touched the molten leather would make any normal person flinch in sympathetic reaction. As they said in the movie, "Biloxi Blues," "It's like Africa hot."

But not as flushed as my face when I suddenly sprawled on the concrete in front of the entrance to the Kentucky Fried Chicken. Have you ever fallen and it feels like slow motion, your arms swinging outward to protect your face from being flattened to the pavement? And, suddenly, the driveway roars up to slap against your hands, biting deeply into your palms?

That day, I realized how exceptionally agile a mature woman can be. I tucked my left shoulder and rolled hard sideways into the decorative rock and thorn bushes. My feet flew straight up in the air, kicking wildly as if I was swimming the American Crawl on a busy sidewalk.

My first thought…who shoved me?

As I lay on my side, scraping purse contents towards my chest, I checked to make sure my silk pants weren't ripped. Thankfully, they only had three-inch-long black tar skid tracks marking the X on each knee. With my inventory complete, personal effects clutched in my hands, I dropped everything back into my purse and slowly climbed to my feet. I abandoned my lunch plans. I had a flight to catch.

I boarded the plane with time to spare and settled into my window bulkhead seat. Within minutes a gray-haired woman sat down next to me and proceeded to intently read her book. Feeling sheepish, I started to rub the tar marks off my knees, hoping that the slacks weren't ruined. The woman glanced over and said, "What happened, sweetie?"

I leaned over and said quietly, "I fell in the parking lot. Stupid."

A stern look crosses her face as she replies, "You didn't just fall. Your angel pushed you. Make the decision." With that, she snapped back to reading her book and did not interact with me for the rest of the trip.

What the hell is she talking about? Angels are supposed to catch people, protect them when they fall. They don't push! I felt my face begin to flush red, not only with embarrassment, but with confusion. The hair on my arms stood up as I stared at this woman so focused on her novel. Did she even speak? Was it something I had imagined?

Her look of righteous indignation at my misinterpreting my fall astounded me, yet, for some reason, it felt correct. The medium had told me to "make the decision." Somehow did this perfect stranger become a messenger used to communicate the angels' wishes?

My denial, hesitation, and second guesses dissipated. Many believe that perfection belongs only to God. All we can do is recognize the battles we fight, from denial to belief, and make our decision to move into the Language of Intentional Contentment.

Chapter 7: Language of Intentional Contentment

How would your life be if you only expected the best outcome? Would you make different decisions or engage in other experiences? We smile when we hear the ageless question, "If you couldn't fail, what would you do?" understanding that failure seems to be built into our DNA.

I have come to think of life as an intricate part of the Tree of Life. As defined by Wikipedia,

> *"The expression Tree of Life was used as a metaphor for the phylogenetic tree of common descent in the evolutionary sense in a famous passage by Charles Darwin (1872). The tree of knowledge, connecting to heaven and the underworld, and the tree of life, connecting all forms of creation, are both forms of the world tree or cosmic tree, according to the Encyclopedia Britannica, and are portrayed in various religions and philosophies as the same tree."*

The Tree of Life concept is based on connecting all forms of creation. While that seems like a broad statement, it must mean that everything is interrelated – heaven, earth, human, and animal.

Is this what might be considered the God connection?

Do we nourish the tree (our lives), or do we work to destroy it, consciously or unconsciously?

Do spontaneous events in our lives define us?

Can we imagine how an event or a day will evolve and then somehow unconsciously play a role in the outcome we expect?

Trying to understand this concept is much like trying to anticipate our reactions to everything we come across. It would mean that we truly know ourselves. So, does that mean that I would have to self-edit everything I do and think to ensure the best possible outcome? What ever happened to spontaneity and letting things happen as they will? Just roll with the punches. What if I forget to duck and get sucker punched?

Look at that, already anticipating and editing.

There is just so much stuff happening around us that if you are anything like me, you sometimes feel like a rabbit in the headlights: standing upright to see what is going on, and then running like hell for cover.

However, the world as we know it doesn't happen like that. Even with all our evaluation and reflection, the world can still catch us by surprise.

Do we have any idea how we might react?

How many times has your day started out innocently enough... the alarm went off like it was supposed to at the right time, the shower temperature calibrated to perfection, and your ride to the airport arrived on time? Check-in at the ticket counter proceeded without any waits or hitches. The clerk even took the time to joke with you!

That is exactly how my day went as I arrived at the Memphis airport. Wandering through the concourse, I purchased a couple of magazines that really interested me and received a great compliment on my stylish glasses. All this before 6:30 AM! I relished the thought of an uneventful day.

Settling down at the gate, I glanced around to identify where the restrooms were located. What I didn't expect to see was a man collapsing onto the hard tile floor as he emerged from the men's room. In one moment, a perfectly groomed, 60-year-old business man had his day ripped away from him without notice. His confident stride terminated without stumble or stagger. He simply dropped to the floor, loose and unconscious. Sitting about 25 feet away, I and the other passengers could hear the back of his head bounce off the tile.

Chapter 7: Language of Intentional Contentment

In that first moment, no one reacted. Then we heard the scream, "Jim!"

We watched as a petite woman surged towards the men's room doorway. Five other men rushed after her, shouting to the clerk in the convenience shop to call 911. The explosion of activity centered on this trauma silenced every voice at the boarding gate.

For ten minutes, the crowd held their breath, offering silent support to this woman who obviously was the man's wife. The airport security and medical staff arrived within minutes to find that the injured man had recovered consciousness and was mumbling. As I boarded the airplane, a gurney arrived and preparations were underway to transport him to a medical facility. I finally let out my breath.

Seeing the face of that woman as she leaped to her feet will stay with me for a very long time. Shock, disbelief, and utter despair rippled across her features as her skin turned a ghastly white. For a moment, I had feared for her as well. In just a second, a completely uneventful, secure day was shattered.

This day evolved into something I didn't expect. During this emergency, I truly understood that we aren't alone. Not alone in the physical sense as well as the spiritual. That our need for connection reaches out, any place and any time, if it is humanly possible.

What remains with me now is a sense of comfort. A security in knowing that I am safe in a crowd, and if I'm not, someone somewhere will try to help.

The Language of Intentional Contentment means that we recognize that our lives are built on a foundation of our creation, like a strong trunk of a tree, to support our family, friends, experiences, dreams, and hopes. Just as a leaf on a tree eventually drops, we lose those we love. But, we still love the smells, colors, and feeling of Autumn because we know after the harsh winter months to come, renewal will begin once again.

A cycle of life, love, and belief that provides comfort.

If we understand our foundations are based in commitment and respect, the objective can be to participate in our lives fully with no regrets. To reach for goals, receive the bounty of our hard work, and change gears as needed without anger or frustration.

My mother used a sledge hammer approach when we had the audacity to complain about a situation. In her eyes, it was deemed as "bellyaching." As a World War II veteran who served as a nurse based in the Philippines, she saw more pain and suffering than a gentle hearted woman should ever experience.

She returned to civilian life determined to make something of herself despite her life's circumstances. Griping about inconsequential things was the same as lobbing a live hand grenade into the conversation. I knew when I shared my sorrow about not being invited to the prom, she was thinking, "At least you still have a hand!"

I'm often humbled by someone else's life experience. It's amazing how others have walked through the most horrifying situations and come out unscathed. Quite frankly, I believe people often hide their scars behind a winsome smile or gentle glance. Sometimes the fact that they are a survivor is worn as a badge of courage. Or perhaps they might find a way to cope by simply not acknowledging the damage they've endured. What startles me the most is when people reveal their scarring in an unabashed, highly visible way.

Many of us have our own horror stories we could share if the timing and circumstance were right. Sometimes our personal traumas seem insignificant when we learn what another human being is experiencing. Perhaps that is why we flock to listen to motivational talks. And strangely, as we listen to the story of woe, we might think to ourselves, "Well, at least I don't have that!" Weird that we can be emotionally comforted by comparing our pain to another's.

To truly respect our connections to each other, it is imperative to stop wishing for those things you want to do. Act!

And therein lies the dilemma. What are we supposed to do now? What does action mean to us and how can those steps be identified and implemented?

Perhaps the following might give you some ideas of actions you can take:

- Do something now to repair relationships.

- Create experiences that improve you as a person.

- Provide support and solace to others.

- Experience heartfelt joy for the moment – lean back and laugh, loud and clear.

- Dance to music – anywhere!

- Engage in a conversation with someone different from you and discover what you have in common.

- Compliment someone and mean it – at least once a day.

- Be of service to someone at least once a day.

Intentional contentment begins with gratitude for what you have. It's not a homework assignment, it's a celebration. You simply enjoy.

Envision this. You have been incredibly busy for the past month. Deadlines loomed, paperwork needed to be completed and contacts made with future clients. Busy is as busy does. Keep that head down and plow through the tasks. That is a day of work well spent.

Except today, you realize you have run out of projects with deadlines. Feeling a bit uncertain, you check your "tasks" list and discover everything is checked off as completed. Nothing scheduled for the next two weeks.

That can't be right.

Next, you go to your contact management software, refresh it so that it displays the most current information and double check those calls and letters that need to go out.

Huh. All done.

Surely that can't be right. But, no, after careful consideration, you realized that you had finally caught up on all your work.

Now what are you supposed to do?

Truthfully, a bit of panic might set in. Until you understand the Language of Intentional Contentment, you might honestly not know what to do with yourself if you are not working on some sort of project.

Of course, you can take an hour off here and there, but work always remains at the end of your "down time" like a treasured friend. And like most of you, when I make time to "relax" all I can think about are the projects that require my attention: new ideas, or anything I think I should be addressing right at that moment. My internal movie queue of good intentions gets longer and longer… requiring me to weed through the recordings and select only those I absolutely want to watch.

Or are you just afraid of what might happen if you stop? Funny thing is, sometimes stopping is doing something! Shut down that laptop, close the office door and…

- Grab a diet soda and a book as you flop down in the big side chair.

- Wander outside and chat with neighbors.

- Play with the dog or hide and seek with the cat.

- Drive to a Dairy Queen and indulge in a Buster Bar.

- Lounge at Starbucks and watch other people buy $5.50 cups of coffee. Perhaps you might hand the barista $20 and ask

Chapter 7: Language of Intentional Contentment

him to apply it to the next few drink orders. Have fun watching the surprised expressions and then be amazed when they "pass on" the good fortune to the next few people in line.

- Stroll through Home Depot and check out the beautiful flowers waiting to be placed on your doorstep.

- Drive by the neighborhood pool and watch your grandchildren swim like little dolphins.

- Go feed the buffalo and elk at the county park.

- Run from bees. At least it is aerobic exercise!

When I wrote those last few lines, I saved the file, and shut down my computer. Rushing out of the office, I spun my husband around in his chair and yelled with delight, "We are going out today and I'm not taking the laptop! What do you want to do or where do you want to go?"

Rick blinked. Being the consummate good sport, he smiled and said, "I don't know...what do you want to do that we both like and can do today?"

I had absolutely no idea. Neither did he.

Ultimately, we jumped into his car and started out with no specific destination in mind. My hands were clenched in my lap as I worked to keep my fingers still. They are so used to typing it is difficult to quiet them. We ended up stopping at local shops we had never taken time to visit. No purpose, just a stroll, hand in hand, checking out what was new in the world. I discovered I hadn't thought about work for two hours. I enjoyed myself so much I didn't want to go home.

> *"If we are to perceive all the implications of the new, we must risk, at least temporarily, ambiguity and disorder."*
> **J.J. Gordon**

Without a specific plan, other than leaving the house and work behind, we discovered aimlessness can result in a destination – contentment! Put simply, we need to value our "down time" as much as we coveted our "busy" times. It becomes a process of breaking the old habit and replacing it with a new pattern of thinking… that what we do can wait for a day while we refuel the mental and physical tanks.

What are you going to do intentionally to create your personal contentment?

If you are uncertain, perhaps this is the moment where listening will help you get to the next step of your journey. The Language of Listening and Responding can offer you a powerful way to reframe how you look at your life and reprioritize it so you live without regret.

Chapter 8: Language of Listening and Responding

The novel you are reading has reached the climatic ending when you look around. What on earth is that? One moment you're contentedly reading a great story and the next this undulating mewl of a cry is echoing across the concourse. Such an odd, piercing noise. Insistent, demanding, and it didn't quite sound quite like an infant's voice.

My guess is you would look around until you identified the source. Forever curious, that is exactly what I did, until I finally observed a tired looking woman, patiently feeding yogurt into the mouth of a child hidden behind a bumper pad in an oversized stroller. Pausing for a moment, the mother drank gratefully from her coffee cup and, for a moment, our eyes met.

It may be our impulse to pass judgement on that mother. Feel a bit ungracious. Why doesn't she keep the kid quiet! Doesn't she know we are already harassed by travel delays? All we ask is a little quiet while we finish our book.

These types of thoughts could come from a need to protect ourselves emotionally through a stressful time. I know, sounds petty, right? And then, when we least expect it, we look up and are confronted with another's reality that can't be ignored. Something shifts in our perception and for a moment, judgement is released and replaced with compassion.

An attitude of resignation floated around the woman, almost palpable in the air-conditioned space. Her expression was so exhausted, I had an urge to speak to her, to take a moment to engage and maybe relieve a bit of her anxiety.

As I approached, I finally peered into the stroller. My heart skipped.

What I saw was a small person laying in the stroller…no more than three feet long. Small, womanly hands grasped at the napkin tucked

45

into a pink sweater. Long brown hair fell in disarray on the bumper pad and pillow. An adult sized nose and large wandering eyes were in complete disproportion to the small chiseled cheekbones and jaw line. Another cry of impatience erupted from the gaping mouth filled with mature teeth, yet the mouth was no larger than that of a six-month old baby.

Constantly scraping portions of yogurt which oozed out of the small person's mouth, the mother whispered words of comfort to the flailing girl.

Time stopped. This woman, a warrior in her own right, had erected an emotional barrier which did not invite interaction with others. The way she held herself, focused only on her coffee and the child screamed the need for solitude. Perhaps it was her way of protecting herself from the curious or possible hurtful comments from insensitive people.

I tell this story because this day I chose to open myself to what was happening around me. I observed and began to make sense of how far I had retreated behind a self-protective barrier. That day, I listened with my heart and responded appropriately to this woman's body language and returned to my seat. I didn't barrel in with both guns blazing, assuming she needed a savior. I respected another's need and acted in a manner I felt she would appreciate.

As I sat back down, I glanced around the gate area and spotted three other mothers hugging and playing with their small daughters – toddlers all. Flushed little cheeks, small legs skipping happily up and down the aisles and the tender hugs signified the absolute joy these children had in just being alive.

Glancing back at the stroller, my heart broke for this woman, isolated from life's simple joys. Her child will never run, talk, or interact normally with her caretakers. Yet, her mother's words of comfort, whispered in a busy public place, seemed to be uttered almost like a talisman against all that is bad in the world. The routine, so practiced and normal, becomes a haven for them both.

Chapter 8: Language of Listening and Responding

Open to observing as much as I could during my short layover, I looked around and noticed a middle-aged man walking slowly toward the row of seats directly in front of me. His broad hand roughly massaged the back of his neck as he sucked down an energy drink. It wasn't his gait or his obvious attempt to revive himself that caught my attention, but his tearful eyes and quivering lower lip.

The man settled down in his seat, eyes darting nervously, giving me the impression he was going to burst into tears. I was convinced that something terrible had happened to him or was about to happen.

Do I get up and offer comfort or ignore him? If he wanted privacy, couldn't he have gone to a restroom? I was torn and uncertain what to do.

Then, out of nowhere, an older gentleman with a leathery wrinkled face, stooped shoulders, and a soft smile, settled in the seat next to the tearful man. As I watched, he leaned over, tapped the younger man on the shoulder and said quietly, "How are things going, big guy?" Startled, the other man's face flushed red, his lower lip trembled and a single tear ran down his cheek. The older man nodded his head and whispered, "I'll be happy to listen if you want to talk. Or, if you prefer, just sit with you for a while." A quiet companionship bloomed between strangers, generated by a person who had room to help shoulder someone else's burden, even if it was for only a short time.

I sighed, humbled and grateful for having witnessed this simple kindness. The Language of Listening and Responding in full force.

Over the years, I've written about good and bad luck, addictions, and other afflictions that are part of the human condition. But, often we lose perspective. Personal and family issues we may experience are transitory; they have a beginning and a foreseeable end. The tired mother with the genetically wounded child must face each day with bravery and strength, if not for herself, for her child. She knows what the morning will bring and she still gets up – over and over again.

Who knows what the story is for the person who weeps publically because something so powerful has overwhelmed their senses? Loss? Fear? Mental illness? We will never know. Each person has their own demons that must be addressed and resolved – but only if their hearts can stand the strain of rising to the challenge.

Over the past few months, I've heard people lament about our world – that it is becoming disconnected, isolated, and people are unwilling to reach out to others. Challenge that point of view – we witness random acts of kindness every day, all around us. And if you are very brave, you too can commit to performing a kind act without any personal gain.

Our human condition is based upon the collective whole, not isolation.

As the 1979 AT&T marketing campaign proclaims, "Reach out and touch someone." You never know what life will show you about yourself in return.

The Language of Listening and Responding is about living fully and having a sense of the world around you. But sometimes tunnel vision becomes a way of life for us.

Have you ever concentrated on something so hard that the world seems to recede into the background? Like when you see a blemish on your chin and it begins to take on the dimensions of a quarter? Or when you are shuffling through a business proposal that you must deliver that day to an unsupportive group of peers? Each, seem to gobble up every inch of brain space as you mull over advantages, consequences, causes, and reactions of others. Our level of anxiety over the mind-numbing details might eventually increase to such an extent that our friends and family become concerned.

When I allow myself to drift into single minded focus, my husband will look at me with an incredulous expression on his face and announce, "You are just not seeing the big picture!" For example, he will begin telling me a story of what happened to a co-worker. As he speaks, my brain locks onto a phrase or portion of the story, working diligently to try and figure out exactly what he means or intends to convey. Rick, however, has already advanced the story line significantly enough that by the time I'm able to re-align my attention, I've missed the whole point of the story.

You see, I've been taught that the devil is in the details and consequently the big picture will take care of itself if I address every single little nuance – such as correcting a spelling error in a love letter sent to me by my fiancé. I think that was the first clue to Rick that our marriage would take on interesting elements.

Essentially, some of us become so focused that we miss what is happening around us. A classic caution in driving is to avoid highway hypnosis where the driver's eyes are so locked onto the road ahead that they don't see what is developing around them; a ripe condition for accidents to happen.

I think we do the same thing in considering the changes we want to make in our personal lives, careers or businesses. When we do strategic planning, all the elements related to our business and personal growth should be evaluated without judgment. Awareness of our surroundings can help us prioritize and focus on "what is" and "what needs to be" in our business decisions.

Perspective is a wonderful thing. We may not like what we see (like an expanding waist line in the mirror), but once we understand what is really happening, only then can we take the necessary steps to fix it or build upon the successes that are already in place. Listen, observe and respond to experiences and information in such a way that you never lose focus on the big picture.

Appreciate nuances of the human mind and capacity of love. Deborah Harkness, author of *The Book of Life*, defined love as follows:

> *You don't need words to tell me what you feel…*
> *I see you even when you hide from the rest of the world*
> *I hear you, even when you are silent*

As I mentioned earlier in this book, my twin brother, Kevin, died March 22, 2016. His body was ravaged as ALS shut down his systems and erased his physical coordination. This highly independent man tried hard to die with dignity. The morning he died, I woke up approximately 30 minutes before his death and felt him call to me and say goodbye.

Vivid dreams? Or that final connection and farewell using all he had left to reach out and move on to whatever awaited him.

Learn to listen not only with your ears, but with your hearts and mind. It will help you hear. Really hear what needs to be received.

We call out to each other, whether friend or stranger, all the time. The God connection is beyond all understanding, but to fully realize your potential, you must master the Language of Action.

Chapter 9: Language of Action

"In our choices lies our fate." Guillermo del Toro

"Make a decision!" My strident internal voice creates a slice of pain that arches over the crown of my head – a jolting order shrieking loudly enough to cause my heart to pound and my face to burn with frustration. It isn't as if I am making a choice between life and death. I must only determine how my business will grow over the next two to five years. Certainly, I can delay mapping out my career until I have a "safe" amount of discretionary cash set aside. Except one thought keeps hounding me: which came first, the chicken or the egg?

Now I understand that it doesn't make any difference which came first. All I must do is commit. No excuses, no lopsided rationalizations that I might not be meant for what I want to do. Just set one foot in front of the other and take the first step. Whether that first step will falter or stride confidently forward is determined by my attitude and strength of belief in my own skills, attributes, and character.

Guillermo del Toro, Hollywood director, carries this phrase with him wherever he goes; *"In our choices lies our fate."* And this is exactly what scares the daylights out of me. All of us have our priorities. No one else sets them for us – we do. We either say "yes!" to a choice or we set it aside. My fear is that I'll say "yes" for all the right reasons, yet find out later that decision set in motion another entirely separate chain of events.

> **It feels like a battleground. And our ancestors look down on us, shaking their heads, wondering when we will figure out that our lives are a constant recalibration.**

Imagine what your life would look like if every day you enjoyed the ultimate in personal experiences – the prospect that your work has value and your career allows you to utilize every skill in your personal arsenal, resulting in an emotional high when others appreciate your efforts. Each effort is rewarded with celebratory kudos and you feel so empowered that you can't wait to do it again the next day. The energy that infuses you makes you giddy with anticipation.

I'm asking you to give in...to stop pushing and turning every day into a battle. Stop trying to force your goals into reality, but intently determine exactly what you want out of your life and act accordingly. What do you *want?*

- More time to explore nature, be with your family, or expand a beloved hobby?
- To build a business that is profitable and will provide you with an acceptable retirement income?
- Become physically fit through a precise schedule of exercise and diet?
- Engage in satisfying work or volunteer activities that make you feel fulfilled in utilizing all your skills and abilities?
- Write a book, song or paint?

Once you determine specifically what you want to have or achieve, then ask for help in creating the environment you want to live in.

Surrender *is* action, because it opens the door for true opportunity. We aren't bulldozing over everything that isn't part of the plan. Instead, we let it grow and possibly blossom into something that will be perfect for you, your family and/or your career. And the big question becomes how does a person do that?

I believe the question really is "what does *thrive* mean to you?" If it's letting everything go for a while and just existing, then that's your answer. Each choice you make sets a path to an outcome. That outcome could take years before it is evident. Take for example my weight gain over 15 years. I chose to eat badly and paid the price. Now my choices are offering other options for me.

Thriving, by definition, means to prosper or flourish; become better than what you were. What that means specifically for each of us can only be measured by where we came from.

A good way to begin is by looking at our past to uncover what we learned and determine how we can use the defeats and successes to increase our opportunities to even *have* the choices we need.

My goal in the Language of Action is to assist you in releasing those sleepless nights of anxiety, and replace them with introspection. Consider these simple questions to explore your way to a successful existence as defined by your intention:

- What three characteristics of my work effort or skill set give me the most satisfaction and what careers value those skills?
- Why can I consider something that utilizes my skills yet can be applied in a different industry?
- Is it really the work that frustrates me or the inability to access my creativity at full throttle? What things can I do outside of work that satisfy that need?
- Who do I know that has attained personal satisfaction in their work and how can I learn from them?
- What specifically would make me happy if money wasn't an issue?
- What responsibilities matter the most to me and why are they important?
- When did I begin to accept that lack of appreciation for my work effort is acceptable? Do I mirror that same philosophy when managing my staff? When did it become okay to not trust and respect the leaders in my company?
- What can I do every day that will help me move toward my goals one small step at a time?
- When I finally reach my goals, what do I expect my life to look like? How will I know I have reached my goals?

The Language of Intent

I want to share a little-known fact about me. It might help explain the Language of Action more clearly.

I used to dance. A lot.

Between the ages of five and fourteen, I remember getting ready to attend my weekly ballet lesson and almost hyperventilating as I slipped my ballet toe shoes into their gray cotton sacks. My excitement had nothing to do with the teacher or the other children, nor the opportunity to admire myself as I grabbed the balance barre that was anchored to the wall of mirrors. I recall the brightly colored tights and the slight haze of baby powder that floated continually in the air from over "freshened" shoes. Sometimes it was so thick I thought I might get covered in the shimmering white dust simply by walking slowly through the hanging cloud.

My joy came from realizing what my body could do when trained properly and tuned to a score of music that lifted the soul. Hefty thoughts for a young girl, don't you think? It was in ballet class that I first heard the William Tell Overture and leapt to unimagined heights powered by the high-speed melody. I learned about grace as I held my arms high over my head during the Blue Danube Waltz. Strength and fierce pride surged out of me as I spun and kicked during the famous Apocalypse Now anthem, Ride of the Valkyries. I teared up at the majesty of a truly beautiful 1812 Overture rising from the instruments of the Boston Pops Orchestra.

The glimpse of a young dancer balanced in a perfect ballet pose on the iconic shuttlecock located on the front lawn of the Nelson-Atkins Museum of Art in Kansas City stopped me in my tracks. I saw myself as I was over 50 years ago. Straight limbed, elegant and full of promise in the world of dance.

Her lines were perfect. And in seeing that perfection, I realized that I had never gotten to that level and it didn't matter. Especially now when the mere thought of lifting my leg higher than my waist causes me alarm. In my aging, I've learned to appreciate fully the talents of others without feeling jealously or regret.

Chapter 9: Language of Action

Dance made me thrive. With my legs, arms, torso, and hips, I would cross a stage in a blur of contained energy and delight. What I still have is the love of music for music's sake.

Sitting in my seat on my flight to Chicago, I listened to Josh Groban singing in his wonderfully melodic tenor voice, and discovered that I was swaying slightly in time to the music. I was also choreographing the dance moves I thought would best represent the soul of the music – all in my head.

And as I contemplate this, I realize I still dance – often in my office accompanied by a barking dog and skittish cats. But I dance the best I can with an appreciation that I still can move.

I used to dance – now I celebrate. What that celebration means is different for each of us. For me, I believe every day is a gift. I'm able to get out of my bed by myself, see the sunlight, listen to new age music on the Pandora station, and pet my cats and dog.

As I mentioned earlier, surrendering to make room for celebration is action. We thrive by feeding the heart, head, and soul. Make your Language of Action focus on thriving, connecting with yourself, and reaching out with intention.

I guess what I'm saying is, "Run, Forrest, run!" from the movie "Forrest Gump." Take the greatest of your experiences and duplicate it – again and again. For me it is the hugs from my grandchildren and gentle smiles from my son as he watches us.

1. Do you look at thriving as a task completed or a celebration that you finished the task with your best ability?
2. Do you do what you love and share that joy with others?
3. Are you like the 80-year-old singer who can still belt out a song with gusto – and on key?
4. Do you explore your genealogy and learn with wonder that your history counts?
5. What would you tell me about the greatest experience you ever had and what it emphasizes in your life?

The Language of Action means that every moment of our lives requires that we make some sort of decision or intention that will set the stage for a true-life event.

Over the past years, I have met more and more individuals who seem frozen in their ability to make decisions of any kind. It's as if their brains have locked into place and they are standing upright wondering where they put the key to their own lives.

Have you ever driven down a strange road without a GPS or the benefit of a map and come to a crossroad? Both roads look equally appetizing and appealing. How does a person choose which direction to turn? Being caught in the middle of an intersection with no desire, direction, or information creates a static environment where nothing seems possible. I believe that is when we begin to settle for what life has given us and we start making assumptions about what comes next.

A few months ago, I was meeting with a successful business owner who, a year previously, has survived a car accident that left him with multiple fractures and a broken back. Within the last few months, some of his close family members had been diagnosed with life threatening illnesses. He looked tired and despondency reeked from every pore in his body. After hearing about his circumstances, I simply asked, "What do you want?"

The question caught him off guard. He rocked back in his chair and his eyes bored into mine. I asked again, "You have been through significant life events in this past year. What do you really want to do now?" He shook his head and told me that he had only been moving forward and hadn't really taken the time to think about what he wanted from his life. He was keeping on top of the day-to-day decisions, but hadn't looked beyond that – at least not until I asked.

Deciding is easier said than done considering all the emotional energy we invest while contemplating our options. Ultimately, we need information and sometimes take the leap of faith much like believing the pronouncements from a crystal ball.

Evaluating possible outcomes to those decisions can be as simple as acknowledging:

1. What is the worst thing that can happen if I make this decision?

2. What is the best thing that can happen if I make this decision?

3. What is most likely to happen if I make this decision?

Once we have these benchmark questions readily in hand, then we can move forward and choose our course. With less time on our hands, we need to make important decisions quickly, though we may be forced to do so with less information than we have had in years past. It is the reality of the world we live in.

If you are at your crossroad, do your due diligence, determine the possible outcomes and then choose. The first step in decision making is always the hardest and often the most anticipated. The reward of your vision becoming a reality just might make your intersection a simple choice in your journey.

Establishing a course of action isn't possible until you can answer these three questions above when you begin planning your next steps.

Some people have such a creative nature, that repetition in the workplace feels like a prison sentence. When the challenges become routine, isn't it natural to look for fulfillment elsewhere? And when we have that urge, at what point do we act on it? That's when the real-world steps in and whispers in our ear all the reasons we need to make do with what we have. The burden of responsibility is a harsh one to bear. But isn't that what adults do?

Our fate and future depends upon how well we know ourselves. Making important decisions can follow a systematized process through the acronym COMMIT:

Calibrate - adjust schedules and projects to balance of business/personal time.

Observe - review personal and business condition for pitfalls. Prioritize their impact.

Manipulate – Move pieces around until a sound path opens.

Memorize – Spend time every morning reviewing goals and updating as needed.

Implement – Begin the building process incorporating flexibility for the unexpected.

Trust – You did your due diligence, so trust your instincts, the plan, and your life partners.

COMMIT is a process that ties into leadership as well as your personal life. Have integrity in your connections and communication style. Be transparent when you can and realize that the element of trust is a vital foundation in building a business or career you can be proud of.

Not to sound overly simplistic, but trust always begins when you are accountable for your attitude and approach to life. When you begin to question with purpose and live with intent, miracles seem to happen. You will discover that you are intentional content – that your mind has the capacity for quiet and your heart beats with the rhythm of possibilities, not threats.

The Language of Intent is already written. It is up to you to make the choices and decisions that will build your foundation of positive self-talk and begin to transform your outcomes.

Chapter 10: Language of Leadership

Leadership means so many different things to so many people. Is it a matter of trust, communication, connection, engagement or accountability? The Language of Leadership is a shifting dialog, but the elements of leadership have remained consistent over the generations. Consider the following…

Dawn is arriving. The chilly air causes the breath of the waiting mass of humanity to materialize as briefly hanging ghostly shapes. Twilight recedes as the sun slowly ascends over the horizon, spearing the darkness with the brilliant light of hope and promise of a new day where anything can happen. Crisp aroma of meadow flowers fills the air and the crowd inhales deeply to capture the scent, if only for a moment.

They wait.

Suddenly, the quiet is shattered by the hammering of a majestic horse's hooves as it gallops over the crest of the hill. Backlit by the rising sun, the anointed leader surges into view and a mighty cheer erupts from the crowd, deafening in the celebration of their chosen leader. Raising a hand, asking for quiet attention, the leader guides the prancing steed, resplendent in silver and highly polished leather, up and down the front lines looking deeply into the eyes of those who have chosen to follow.

After the intense moment of connection, the leader positions the horse so every eye can see him and the sound of the leader's voice carries easily to every woman, man, and child gathered in the meadow.

Eyes flashing, head held high, he speaks.

The voice of authority, possibility, love, and urgency fills the air and those who listen feel their eyes fill with tears, too enraptured to hold back any emotion. This is the day when we fight for our freedom.

Independence Day.

At least that is how the movies and books say leadership looks and feels. This rousing, intense interaction between leader and follower is natural and logical. But, let's re-run the scenario again for today's environment:

Twilight is arriving. All company employees move quickly into the corporate lobby. Through the rain-streaked windows, employees witness the sun as it descends behind the skyline, obscured by smog. A day is ending, where each employee knows anything can happen. The smell of panicked sweat permeates the air.

They wait.

Suddenly, the murmur of the assembly is shattered by the elevator door opening one story above at the atrium level. Backlit by the florescent light, the president of the company calmly walks up to the railing and looks down over the crowd. Raising a hand, asking for quiet attention, the leader, looking tired and pale, gazes sadly into the eyes of those who have been hired to work for his company.

Choosing a location at the railing where every eye can see him, the sound of the leader's voice carries easily to every woman and man. The voice of authority and urgency fills the air and those who listen feel their eyes fill with tears, too shocked to hold back emotion. This is the day when they are given their freedom – released from their jobs due to the recession.

Independence Day.

Both scenarios highlight a leader who can stand and deliver the best and worst of news with compassion and strength. Harsh, necessary decisions are the responsibility of a leader; delivering the results of those decisions to members who follow with trust and commitment is one of the hardest things a leader will ever do.

Could this be why fewer people are willing to assume the mantle of leadership, even if it only involves personal responsibility?

Chapter 10: Language of Leadership

Leadership is placed on our shoulders in all sorts of ways; group acclimation, recognition of a job well done, or as a logical progression in the scheme of things. Often, we receive the benefit of ascension to a position of power through financial rewards, perks, public recognition, and the ability to create necessary change. That must sustain us at night when we have trouble sleeping.

Many leaders feel isolated because they choose to keep power and information firmly within their grasp, afraid that any leak of bad data would cause anxiety in the workforce and negatively impact productivity. Isn't the leader supposed to be strong enough to stand alone?

Let's go back to the movie scenario. This leader exudes confidence in her followers, an undying faith that they will understand the issues at hand, work with her to solve the problem through group interaction, even if that means charging toward a destination that could result in destruction. At least they did it together.

> **The role of the leader isn't about isolation. It's about creating such a powerful presence within a group that people choose to follow, knowing their voices will be heard, considered, and implemented when it makes sense.**

Because they trust their leader and the integrity of the connection between both sides, the members commit to the direction the leader is taking and have faith in the outcome, willingly giving up their independence for a greater good.

The power of leadership is in collaboration. When that happens, anything is possible, even in the harshest of times. Ultimately it boils down to your willingness and ability to be an effective mentor. You'd think I would learn the best lessons from the corporate or association worlds. My best mentor has been my husband. Who knew?

Rick has a pained expression on his face as he watches me try to catch a piece of paper that had escaped our car in the parking lot. I would approach the paper slowly (in stealth mode, like a lion advancing on its prey), only to have a sudden gust of wind whisk it upward and out of my reach. After a few failed attempts, he finally shouts "Just run up to it and step on it!"

The man's a genius. Mission accomplished with the next attempt.

Mentoring is much like that: watching another person try to accomplish a task without much success and then stepping in to offer a suggestion that makes all the difference in the world. Now if we would only become more proactive in preventing problems... Technically, the mentoring moment with Rick should have happened before the paper blew out of our car. A small suggestion that I gather up my trash prior to opening my door on a very windy day would have eliminated my need to act like a ninja in broad daylight.

Being a mentor is a quiet way of building a coaching relationship. Consider a baby duck learning to swim for the first time. They watch the mother duck slip effortlessly into the water as they dance on one foot then the other before making the leap of faith to follow suit. The calm confidence of their mother and mentor provides a foundation from which to leap into unknown territory.

Setting aside time on a regular basis to evaluate progress with your mentor can be extremely satisfying and productive, especially when the exchange of information is a two-way street between you and a younger person. We might just see the magic in having a different point of view, which gives us the extra push to incorporate new thoughts and perspectives into our problem-solving process. With our world changing in an exponential manner due to technology and social issues, that moment to sit down and breathe can be rewarding on many levels.

Take a chance and approach someone you respect and admire and ask if they would consider being your mentor. If they say yes, follow these five tips to enhance that relationship:

1. **Set a regular scheduled meeting time and place**. The amount of time doesn't have to be significant, but should be

long enough to explore a topic fully before having to pack up and leave.

2. **Never waste your mentor's time.** Identify the main reason for your meetings and, if necessary, create an agenda in advance. Knowing what will be discussed will not only help your mentor to prepare, but also you will be able to cover twice the territory in your allotted time.

3. **Do what you promised to do.** Nothing frustrates a mentor or coach more than ignoring the tasks you promised to complete before the next meeting. Sure, sometimes circumstances make it unavoidable, but a consistent pattern of making promises and breaking them will end a mentoring relationship quickly and possibly forever. All you must do is meet your mentor half way.

4. **Select topics that reinforce your strengths.** Spend time using the advice from your mentor to build your competence to a higher level. Much of what you will learn will center on "approaches" to problem solving. The more you understand your strengths, the more effectively you can incorporate the advice from your mentor.

5. **Provide value back to your mentor.** As the mentoring relationship deepens, you will begin to realize you also have advice and experiences to share with your mentor. Never fail to ask, "How can I be of service to you?" Your mentor may never ask anything of you, but they will always remember that you offered. That is huge.

I consider my marriage as one big mentoring relationship. No one knows me better than my spouse and child. He's much more proactive with me now and gives me advice before something happens. That's a lesson we learned when Rick watched me vigorously dry a wet cookie sheet with a cotton towel when we were first married. He called my name, getting ready to suggest I lighten my touch.

I turned my head to look at him which in turn caused me to take my eye off the towel. My hand slipped off the top of the cookie sheet which was bent away from me. Like a cartoon noise, a resounding "whap" filled the kitchen as the cookie sheet slammed into my head. Dazed, I looked to my husband for support and advice.

Rick, in his best mentoring voice, offered this observation… "At least it wasn't a frying pan."

Priceless.

Chapter 11: Language of Intent

Did you happen to notice that the older we get, the less likely it is that we allow ourselves to play in the moment? How many times have you been mischievous and the other person looks balefully at you and says, "Grow Up!"

When did having to grow up become synonymous with being serious and mature?

Okay, I'll acknowledge there is a time and place for being an adult, such as during a church service or attending a business meeting regarding the financial future of a company. But have we forgotten that humor and fun surround us every day and all we need to do is recognize it and lean in to play? I find that using humor during a conversation or an offhand remark is my way of gauging whether the person I'm talking to still has a sense of fun.

I'm not talking about razzing someone to the point that it is hurtful. But speaking an obvious truth in such a way that others can see the turn of phrase and enjoy the moment for what it is. Just plain fun.

For example, during a conversation at a convention luncheon, one attendee announced to the table that they were going to follow me wherever I went as they wanted to learn as much as they could from me. First, I was highly flattered and my grin told her that. But what came out of my mouth was "So, are you announcing that you are going to be stalking me? Should I expect you to photo bomb me everywhere I go during this conference?" Her eyes lit up and said, "If that is what it takes, I'm game!" Throughout the day she took every opportunity to stand next to me and behind others and hold up her phone.

What a hoot!

She played the entire day and I couldn't wait to see what she would do next. The look of sheer delight in her face made it extra fun for me and those around her.

50 years old and she still has it.

As adults, we just are more limited in how we play. If we act too juvenile, we might be considered senile and forced into some sort of psychiatric treatment. My husband almost considered this when I decided to only talk like a monkey after watching "Greystoke – Tarzan of the Jungle" years ago. In the movie, the realistic looking apes made a cooing, "ooh…. ooh..." sound and used the backs of their hands to stroke their loved ones. I proceeded to do that in the privacy of our home – cooing over him as he cooked, or sat on the couch beside me. I even started parting his hair looking for fleas. Yup, I did that.

Each time I play like a monkey, I crack up laughing. He would look at me with a blank expression and sigh. My son picked up on the play and became baby monkey. For two days, if anyone had looked through a window and observed us, the white van would have been ordered.

Have you ever played hide and seek with your cat? I've owned five Siamese cats in my life and every one of them responded to and came to their name, and would actively play hide and seek with me. For example, my cat Stryder would chase me down the hall, slap my leg as if to tag me as "it" and then race away to a place of hiding. I go in search to his favorite spots, pat him on the rear end and run away. Within seconds, he creeps down the hall looking for me behind doors and around corners – only to begin the cycle again. If you were outside listening through open windows, I'm sure the thundering trod of my shoes, the quick patter of cat's feet and my shrieks of laughter would make you wonder about my sanity.

Recently, I watched a small boy sit on the floor of an airport terminal gift shop proceed to pull two stuffed toys off the rack and begin to do battle. The bunny rabbit was losing to Mickey Mouse and his sheer concentration on his imaginary world was a delight to behold.

The Language of Intent is to find those moments of play in your life – the world is serious enough already.

Chapter 11: Language of Intent

Play like you mean it!

- Be silly – wear bright colored socks or mismatched clothes.
- Go with a friend and try on wigs. The uglier the better.
- Dress up as a bag lady and show up at work. As a supervisor in an insurance company in Minneapolis, I did exactly that years ago. Copied the look of Laugh In's Ruth Buzzi, hair net and all, with a half-smoked lady cigar dangling out of my mouth. Ended up being ushered out of the building three times by security before the CEO recognized me. Laughed about it for days and lifted spirits in my department at a highly stressful time.
- Walk the mall and see how slow you can go.
- Try on a tube top and try to make it stay up. As a woman who is not well endowed, it would roll down to my waist with a simple move of my hips. Invited my husband into the dressing room and we howled with laughter. Loud enough that, yes, we were asked to leave.
- Put a label inside your custom leather purse that says it is a road kill purse.
- Go up to a high intensity fan and talk through the blades so that your voice sounds like a robot.
- Inhale helium whenever and wherever you can.
- Pay for someone else's dinner when they don't expect it. Better yet, do it for a stranger and leave before they know it is paid for.
- Spend the afternoon petting animals at the animal shelter.

When was the last time you really felt you were living a blessed life? When I ask this of individuals I meet throughout the country, some of the answers are quite revealing:

"I can't remember when…"

"Haven't had the time to think about that - I'm too busy living"

"When I held my newborn child, twenty years ago."

"When I made enough money to cover my bills last month"

"When I woke up from a life-threatening surgery a year ago and every day since."

People came at the question from such different angles. Some focused entirely on the here and now, while others looked for extreme moments in their lives that changed their perception of life in general. What is taken away from every response is that life is too short to wonder "what if?" At what point do we finally begin to attack the bucket list and start filling our hearts with life experiences that we value?

I find it astounding the way young people manage to travel around the world on a dime. They are willing to experience discomfort in accommodations to have the experience of a lifetime. Mark LeBlanc, two years ago, walked The Way, planning the pivotal experience for years before he departed on one of the most uplifting periods of his life. He is walking it for the second time as I write this book. I've been in awe of his decision ever since I heard about it.

How does the Language of Intent work in relationship to second chances?

Let me share a quick story about Linda; her face registered complete frustration and helplessness. The grayish tint of her skin announced to everyone that she was under a great deal of stress. For the past hour, Linda had shared her utter disappointment in the life she had led and announced that she would give anything for a second chance.

- A second chance to make different decisions and choices.
- A second chance to share her feelings truthfully to those she loved and lost.
- A second chance to make a career move that seemed completely implausible.

Chapter 11: Language of Intent

What is saddest of all? This woman knows that wishing for second chances is unproductive and solves nothing. But the *idea* of a second chance is what appeals to her; the concept that she can erase everything that has occurred previously and begin anew.

After this exhausting conversation, I decided to watch two movies that are based exactly on this concept: *Family Man* with Nicholas Cage and the *Butterfly Effect* with Ashton Kutcher. One movie involves an angel that allows a high powered lonely business executive to live the life he could have had if he had taken a different path; the other has our "hero" using his psychic abilities to move backward in time and change his behavior to achieve his preferred outcome.

Upon viewing them again, I had a reinforced commitment to live my life without regret, which is what I believe the desire to activate a second chance is all about. Without divine intervention or a super mental ability, none of us can shift time to accommodate our regret.

What has happened happened. Period. How we respond to a decision or an outcome is what shapes our future and sets us up for future decisions. Do you believe it is human nature to think we can control outcomes? Or do you believe that all we can do is control how we respond to stress, anger, opportunity or sorrow? Which leads me to wondering how do we stop making unfortunate choices? Is it possible to direct our lives without being bombarded with outside influences?

As my mother used to say, "Get real." Her adamant commitment to the stark realities of cause and effect shaped my decision-making process. When I had those soul searching discussions with her, she would reply "If you make this decision, you must live with the consequences, which means always prepare for the worst possible thing that may occur as a direct result of that decision." She would then remind me that my life is more than today. It is a direct accumulation of experiences that will shape the person I will become.

I recognize and have experienced truly horrible things. But if we constantly remind ourselves about the joy and wonder that surrounds us it might be entirely possible to regain a balanced perspective. I know I have said things I wish I could take back, so I do the next best thing: I ask forgiveness and try to restate my comment in a way that isn't hurtful or painful to the other person. What they choose to do with that apology is entirely up to them. That is something I can't control, but at least I know I tried.

I put the intention out to the universe that I want to mend the relationship and will do anything I can to make that intention become real. Consciously thinking about the intention created unconscious decisions that move me toward the goal I am seeking to reach.

Our intention regarding our lives requires that we consider what is in our hearts and truly understand *what we want*. We can't keep waiting for that moment that will solve all our problems, or that solution that bridges the gap from a bad situation to a breathlessly great outcome.

To heal your heart is something only you can do with purposeful intent. Look beyond the pain and focus on the outcomes which are of value to you and yours.

>**Engage honestly and consistently.**
>
>**Connect meaningfully.**
>
>**Live and breathe transparency, which ultimately leads to trust because you are authentically you.**

We learn so much from others who are part of our families. As you might have guessed, my mother was a powerful influence on me as well as my older sister, Kendall. Two powerful, self-reliant women who both demonstrated a boundless capacity for love and taking care of their respective worlds. Each chose to address her trials in different but no less impactful ways. Both are individuals who modeled my understanding of the Language of Intent and the power of self-talk.

Chapter 11: Language of Intent

The most powerful wisdom my mother imparted happened in her passage from life. As my mother lay dying, she clutched my husband's hand and asked him if he had any regrets about his life or actions he had taken.

A bit startled, Rick looked at her with utmost kindness and said "Absolutely none. I wouldn't be the man I am today if I hadn't made the choices I did."

With teary eyes, she weakly lifted her hand and touched his cheek, patted it sharply and replied with a soft smile…

"Good man. You've been listening."

- If there is someone you need to reconnect with or apologize to – call them.

- If there is someone who needs your help but doesn't know how to ask for it – step up.

- If there is someone who needs your strength – stand strong.

Second chances exist in your next decisions. Choose wisely.

The Language of Intent has some simple rules to live by. The process of moving through and embracing the truth of each of the life languages I have introduced is methodical, reachable and enduring.

Live on.

Live boldly.

Live with intent.

Chapter 12: Observations of Simple Life Rules

With decades of interacting with people, teaching, mentoring and being mentored, problem-solving and tackling whatever life flings at me under my belt, lessons can't help but be learned. The voices of men and women across the country teach me every day about the realities of a full life. The map has been laid out for you in this book. Perhaps these recommendations and observations can give you additional road markers for your journey to intentional contentment.

- Live like you mean it. Don't squander your time unless there is a purpose, such as recharging your batteries.

- Laugh. When you laugh, it leaves less room for self-pity.

- Tell others that you love them. People can't read minds; they need to hear it.

- Respectful discourse is your right. Don't be afraid to share your feelings. Good or bad, they mean something to you.

- No dream is too big or outrageous. The world has a way of aligning itself to a person's vision. It creates an energy which is defined by belief in the possible.

- When you have a passion for something…pursue it.

- Stay healthy. Be observant and diligent in resolving problems.

- Be a truthful person, especially when looking at yourself.

- Help others to reach their dreams – be a positive collaborator.

- Work and make friends with good people. If you don't respect the people you are most closely associated with, get out.

- Your integrity is who you are. Protect it at all costs.

- Give people the benefit of the doubt. Evaluate the transgression, get to the truth and then act accordingly.

- Seek answers. Keep asking questions until you are satisfied or have a true understanding of a situation. Perspective is critical. Go to the source.

- Live for no regrets when it comes to family matters. You only have one Mom and Dad. Do what you can, when you can to maintain at least some semblance of contact. When they are gone, at least you will know that you did everything in your power to create a relationship that was healthy in some measure.

- Build a long-term relationship with someone who respects and values you. This individual should make you want to be the best possible human being. Just knowing that person exists for you will make your life trials manageable.

- Try something new. You never know what you will discover.

- Live your life with excitement, not fear. Cowering from risk, backing away from a confrontation that could improve your situation are all elements of personal fear. Live with your arms wide open, ready to embrace what comes your way. You can always shove it back out of your life if it isn't a good fit.

- Remember your personal history. We have a way of repeating ourselves without even realizing it.

- We all have guardian angels on our shoulders. Try to be one in life.

- Don't ever, ever say it can't be done. If you are willing to work hard enough, learn, invest, and apply yourself, you can achieve goals that others might think are unreachable. Your best revenge is to succeed.

Unfurl

There was a time when I thought, "That's all there is."

There was a time when I believed I had no more to give.

There was a time that I learned that all my joy could fade,

And every hand and trick I knew had already been played.

It's guaranteed that my heart bleeds at a harshly spoken word,

And something dies – a small weak cry, a young soul submerged.

Then you offered your hand, warming this hollow heart of tin

Which blares a new song, singing, "hope abounds" and I softly join in.

Now shines the day when I decide it's time to join the game,

And in my heart, a new calm state, I release all blame.

The choice is mine! To charge the door with my life to find

No more a gray world, I slowly unfurl, a treasured loving mind.

I expand on out.

Breath in and shout

Burst through the barriers

And stand.

Written by Karel Murray for the 6-year-old in the basement.

Resource Bonus Page

Ask questions about your business and personal life. Explore more deeply what you value and what your intentions are for all levels of your life. Take a moment to delve into and define the specifics that make of the languages of your life. Perhaps with this gentle prod, you will stop saying "yeah, but" and begin to think "yes, and…"

Career

1. What does your financial landscape look like? How much control do you have over your finances?
2. What amount of funds or business do you need to survive through an economic downturn and how much do you need to thrive? What resources do you have available to you to shore up your financial portfolio?
3. Can you build expertise, expand the hours you work, or change to a more lucrative occupation? What have other individuals experienced and does that mirror what is happening to you?
4. Once you have an accurate depiction of how your financial portfolio is developing, begin to address areas to update, change or enhance. Consider http://www.YourBestMoneyMoves.com
5. How is your business impacted by turnover?
6. Is your time taken up in orienting new hires or actively working to maintain key employees in terms of running your business?
7. Is your staff working at optimum levels and enjoying the work they do?
8. If you are an entrepreneur, are your physical and mental resources charged up and in good working condition? Often our personal energy overrides the physical or mental exhaustion we may feel and you may not even be aware your engine is slowing down. Take a personal inventory and do what you must to retain your vitality.
9. Realistically evaluate what you offer in terms of product or services and determine if the marketplace still wants it. Even

though you feel the public needs what you have, a fickle public will purchase what it wants and may leave you behind.

10. Interview other entrepreneurs, professionals, and current and past clients for real time information. Decisions made in a vacuum are never a good thing.
11. Evaluate what steps you need to take to catch up with current technology in social networking, online meetings, and equipment/communication tools. Even though technology continues to evolve daily, you can utilize resources that meet your needs currently and through the next couple of years.

Personal

1. What are my life goals?
2. How do I feel when I am living my goals?
3. I would like my life to be like...
4. What were the last five choices I made that gave me a sense of autonomy in my life?
5. To me, a peak period of happiness is when...
6. If I were to leave my job, how would others remember me?
7. What actions/decisions have I taken/made in my life where I knew there would be an adverse outcome, but I did it anyway?
8. What actions or decisions have I made where there was some adverse outcome that I did not anticipate?
9. After such an adverse outcome, did it become "obvious" that such an outcome could have been predictable?
10. When I die, what do I want to be remembered for and why?

About the Author
Karel Murray

An accomplished author and humorist, Karel presents nationally and internationally.

Enjoy her other books:

- *Conquering the Witch Within: Intergenerational Work Place Strategies that Get Results*
- *Hitting Our Stride: Women, Work, and What Matters*
- *Straight Talk: Getting Off the Curb.*

Karel is a featured author in:

- *Extreme Excellence: Dynamic Interviews with America's Top 10 Performance Experts*
- *Ovation: How to Present Like a Pro by Len Elder*
- *Crystalline Moments: Discover Your Opportunities and Create Your Best Self by Coni Meyers*
- *My Glasses Are on Top of Your Head: Tales of Life, Longevity and Laughter by Brenda Elsagher*

Karel holds a BA in human resources and has earned numerous designations and certifications, including the prestigious National Speakers Association CSP (Certified Speaking Professional) and the Real Estate Educators Association DREI (Distinguished Real Estate Instructor).

Her résumé includes experience as a human resources regional executive of a large commercial insurance firm, as an award-winning salesperson, as a manager of a top-producing real estate office, and as owner of Our Branch, Inc., a national and international speaking and training company.

Lightning Source UK Ltd.
Milton Keynes UK
UKHW010437180119
335758UK00006B/623/P